Family and Succession Law in Ireland

Family and Succession Law in Ireland

Fourth Edition

Paul Ward

This book was originally published as a monograph in the International Encyclopaedia of Laws/Family and Succession Law.

Founding Editor: Roger Blanpain
General Editor: Frank Hendrickx
Volume Editor: Walter Pintens

Wolters Kluwer

Published by:
Kluwer Law International B.V.
PO Box 316
2400 AH Alphen aan den Rijn
The Netherlands
E-mail: lrs-sales@wolterskluwer.com
Website: www.wolterskluwer.com/en/solutions/kluwerlawinternational

Sold and distributed by:
Wolters Kluwer Legal & Regulatory U.S.
7201 McKinney Circle
Frederick, MD 21704
United States of America
E-mail: customer.service@wolterskluwer.com

ISBN 978-94-035-4893-7

e-Book: ISBN 978-94-035-4634-6
web-PDF: ISBN 978-94-035-4644-5

The Author

Paul Ward was born on 25 June 1965, in Somerset, England. He studied law at University College Dublin, where he graduated with a BCL in 1987. He continued his legal studies at the Honourable Society of King's Inns from where he graduated in 1989 as a qualified barrister and was called to the Irish Bar. Paul then studied for a Master's at the London School of Economics and Political Science, where he graduated with an LLM. (European Studies) in 1991. He practised as a barrister at the Irish Bar for a number of years before joining the Faculty of Law at University College Dublin in 1992.

Since 1992, Paul has held the academic posts of Assistant Lecturer (1991–1996) and College Lecturer (1996–2005). He is currently an Associate Professor and Programme Director for Business and Law degree at UCD Sutherland School of Law. He has published domestically and internationally on family law and child law issues.

The Author

Table of Contents

List of Abbreviations

I. Officers

A-G	Attorney General
C.J.	Chief Justice
DPP	Director of Public Prosecutions
J.	Judge
JJ.	Judges
P.	President (High Court)

II. Common Terms

Art./Arts	Article (of the Constitution)
cf.	compare with
ch./chh	chapter/chapters
cl/cll	clause/clauses
Co.	Company
ed./eds	editor/editors
ed.	Edition
e.g.	for example
etc.	*et cetera*
ibid.	*Ibidem*
i.e.	*id est*
Ltd.	limited company
n/nn	note/notes (footnotes)
No.	number
para./paras	paragraph/paragraphs
reg./regs	regulation/regulations (Ministerial Orders or Statutory Instruments)
s./ss	section/sections
sub-s/sub-ss	sub-section/sub-sections
Unreported	Unreported decision of the High Court or Supreme Court
vol.	volume

List of Abbreviations

III. Common Cited Irish Law Reports

IR	Irish Reports
Ir.	Jur. Rep Irish Jurist Reports
ILRM	Irish Law Reports Monthly
ILTR	Irish Law Times Reports
Fam	LJ Family Law Journal

IV. Common Cited Other Law Reports

AC	English Law Reports, Appeal Cases
All	ER All England Reports
Ch	English Law Reports, Chancery
ECHR	European Court of Human Rights
ER	English Reports
F	English Law Reports, Family
FLR	Family Law Reports Fam Family
KB	English Reports, King's Bench
P	English Law Reports, Probate
QB	English Reports, Queens Bench
TLR	Times Law Reports
WLR	Weekly Law Reports

General Introduction

Chapter 1. General Background of the Country

1. The population of Ireland based on the last census in 2016 was 4,784,000. The estimated population of the capital city Dublin is 544,107 individuals.

2. The Irish climate is generally mild with temperatures varying from 7°C in January to 19°C in July. The average daily sunshine in December is two hours, increasing to six hours in June. The average monthly rainfall is between 2 and 3 inches.

3. The total landmass area of Ireland is 84,412 sq. km and the total distance of the coastline is 3,172 km. Ireland is comprised of four provinces: Leinster in the east, Munster in the south, Connaught in the west, and part of Ulster in the north. The four provinces are divided amongst twenty-six counties and when combined with the six counties of Northern Ireland constitute thirty-two counties in total. The six counties of Northern Ireland do not form part of the State of Ireland. The highest mountain, a mere 1,041 m high, is known as Carrantouhill in County Kerry. The Shannon is the longest river stretching some 340 km. The largest lake, Lough Corrib, is situated in the west of the State and is 45 km in length with a total area of 17,612 sq. km and contains 365 islands. The scenery of Ireland is unique and often spectacular. Wild bog lands in mountain and lowland areas provide distinctive natural habitats to life forms. As an island nation, biodiversity of wildlife is low and many indigenous mainland European species are absent from this State. Common plant and animal forms arrived by human settlers.

4. The national language of Ireland is 'gaeilge' (Gaelic or Irish) but English is the everyday language of use by the vast majority of the population. The Irish language evolved from the arrival of Celtic immigrants around 600 BC. The language still survives today in spite of Viking and Norman invasions. The English language was introduced by the Normans and slowly became commonly used in both administrative and legal business. As a consequence, the Irish language became the language of the poorer classes and from the eighteenth century onwards English became and is the general vernacular. The Irish Constitution guarantees freedom of religion to all. The majority religious belief is Roman Catholicism, but in recent years wide and diverse cultural and religious diversity has occurred mainly through immigration, asylum seekers, and refugees.

5. Historically, 7000 BC can be identified as the earliest date when settlers from Britain arrived in Ireland. By 3000 BC, the Stone Age or Neolithic people arrived and their stone monuments are evident today across the landscape. In 2000 BC, Bronze-Age metalworkers arrived in Ireland. The Patron Saint of Ireland, St. Patrick, arrived in 432 AC and converted the pagan Gaelic kings to Christianity, often fabled in the concept of St. Patrick driving snakes from Ireland. Within a century, Irish missionaries were spreading Christianity throughout Europe. The Vikings invaded and plundered around 800 AD, and by 914 AD they began to settle mainly near the South Coast. Intermarriage, trading, and fighting between the Vikings and the native Irish ensued until 1014 AD when the High King of Ireland, Brian Boru, at the Battle of Clontarf, defeated an army of Vikings. The next most significant event in Irish history occurred in 1541 AD when King Henry VIII declared himself King of Ireland, which led to the 'planting' of Ireland with English and Scottish settlers. The 'Plantation of Ireland' caused considerable unrest amongst the native Irish and resulted in the 'Nine Years War' and defeat for the Earl of Tyrone, Hugh O'Neill, in 1601 at the Battle of Kinsale, even with the assistance of the Spanish Armada. In 1872 AD, the Irish Parliament was granted independence from England and some of the Penal Laws, which discriminated against Catholics, were repealed. Daniel O'Connell founded the Catholic Association in 1823 AD and by 1829 AD, Catholic Emancipation removed the vast majority of restrictions imposed on Catholics.

6. The first government of the modern independent Irish State was formed in 1923. According to Article 4 of the Constitution, the official name of the Irish State is 'Éire'. The National Flag is a tricolour formation of green, white, and orange. The National Anthem is entitled 'Amhrán Ná bhFiann' or 'The Soldier's Song'. The National Public Holiday is St. Patrick's Day on 17 March, which is celebrated in many countries around the world.

7. The fundamental laws of the State are contained in '*Bunreacht na hÉireann*', or the Constitution, which defines Ireland as a sovereign, independent, and democratic State. The Constitution provides for the administration of government, defines legal and social policy, and guarantees fundamental rights for citizens. Ireland has a President elected by the people but the role is ceremonial rather than executive in nature. The President has certain powers conferred by the Constitution.

8. The Government is led by the Taoiseach (Prime Minister) and consists of no less than seven members and no more than fifteen nominated by the Taoiseach. The deputy to the Taoiseach is known as the Tánaiste. Departments of State are managed by Ministers appointed by the Taoiseach, and a Minister may manage more than one Department of State.

9. Ireland is a democratic State and the National Parliament is known as the Oireachtas and consists of the President and two houses, the Dáil (The House of Representatives) and the Seanad (Senate). The Dáil is the primary of the two houses in which debate on government administration and policy occurs.

10. Irish law is based upon the common law and the fundamental principles provided for in the 1937 Constitution. Apart from domestic law promulgated by the Oireachtas, statutes passed by the British Parliament prior to 1921 still have the force of law unless repealed or declared unconstitutional. Fundamental to Irish law is the requirement that justice be administered in public as provided for by Article 34 of the Constitution.

Chapter 2. Historical Background of the Irish Legal System, Family Law, and Succession Law

§1. Emergence of the Irish Legal System

11. At the basis of the Irish legal system is the common law. The common law was established in England following the Norman invasion in 1066 and Ireland was the next country to be invaded by the Normans in 1169. It took until the seventeenth century for the common law to take a stronghold in Ireland as the primary legal system. Originally the King of England was the law-making authority. The establishment of the King's justices was the basis for the development of the common law in England and subsequently in Ireland. The first proper establishment of the rule of English law in Ireland came in 1494 with Poyning's Law, which declared that no separate Irish Parliament could be established to legislate for Ireland unless there was Royal consent to such. Poyning's law only took effect in the eastern part of the country known as the 'Pale'. Outside this area, Brehon law continued to be applied. Between the mid-sixteenth century and the seventeenth century, the English rule of law spread to the remaining parts of Ireland mainly due to King Henry VIII's system of Plantation. This involved taking land from the native Irish landowners and granting it to English and Scottish settlers. For a brief period in 1783, Ireland had its own Parliament, known as 'Grattan's Parliament', and legislated for its citizens until 1800. Grattan's Parliament was disbanded in 1800 with the Act of Union following a revolution in 1798 that was motivated by the French and American revolutions at that time. The common law continued to develop over the centuries by the judiciary making decisions and formulating the law. The English Parliament governed Ireland until 1922 when the Irish Free State was established, and the English Parliament remained in force until the introduction of the current Constitution in 1937.

12. During the nineteenth century, the origins of the current system of democratic government were developed in England. Parliament gradually assumed authority to pass laws, and Royal involvement lessened in the process. At this time, the executive assumed the legislative authority of the King, authority which was administered by the Crown's Ministers. The role of the judiciary also developed.

13. During the nineteenth century, the common law and chancery courts were fused with the passing of the Supreme Court of Judicature; this happened in 1873 for England and in 1877 for Ireland. The common law courts administered commercial matters and the chancery court matters concerning land. The division between the two systems was not very clear. In Ireland, the Judicature Act, 1877 established the High Court of Justice, which was divided into four courts and from which the name of the courts in Dublin is taken. The four courts were the Court of Exchequer, which dealt with disputes in relation to the King's Treasury; the court of Common Pleas, which dealt with private civil claims; the Court of King's/Queens Bench, which dealt with criminal and civil matters; and the Court of Chancery, which determined equitable matters. There were other divisions of the High Court of Justice in such areas as Admiralty, Landed Estates, Bankruptcy; Probate, and

Matrimonial Causes and Matters. The House of Lords operated as a court of final appeal from these courts. There were inferior courts in the legal system. These were the Assize Courts, which was a travelling court and determined criminal and civil cases. The Quarter Session Court sat four times a year and heard less serious criminal matters than the Assizes. The Petty Session Court determined preliminary matters for the Quarter Session court. Finally, the County courts determined civil matters of a minor nature.

14. The Home Rule Movement of the late nineteenth century sought to establish an independent State for Ireland. The movement culminated in the Home Rule Act, 1914, which provided for an independent Parliament for what was to become the Irish Free State but which was suspended due to the outbreak of World War I. The nationalist movement launched a revolution in 1916, which was repressed but which ultimately achieved an independent Parliament for the Irish Free State. The rebellion resulted in the establishment of a provisional government and parliament, Dáil Eireann, which assumed authority to legislate on behalf of the people of the new Irish Free State. The Government of Ireland Act, 1920 divided Ireland into two jurisdictions: the Republic of Ireland and Northern Ireland. Each jurisdiction was to have its own Parliament and court system. The provisional government negotiated the Anglo-Irish Treaty in 1921 with the British government, which conferred independence upon Ireland but which meant that the Irish Free State was to remain part of the Commonwealth. The decision to accept the Anglo-Irish Treaty led to division amongst the provisional government and this in turn led to a civil war that lasted until 1923.

15. The Constitution of the Irish Free State was introduced in 1922 and provided for the establishment of the High Court of Justice and a Supreme Court. The current courts system was established by the Courts of Justice Act, 1924 and provided for the establishment of the District Court, the Circuit Court, the High Court, and the Court of Criminal Appeal, which determined appeals from the Circuit and High courts in criminal matters. A Supreme Court was provided for determining which court is the court of final appeal. A Court of Appeal was established on 28th October 2014.

16. This system remained in force until the passing of the Constitution in 1937, Bunreacht na hEireann. This repealed the 1922 Constitution and provided for a new court system which was essentially the same as that provided for in the 1922 Constitution. The Irish Free State became what is now known as the Republic of Ireland. The Courts (Supplemental Provisions) Act, 1961 provided for the establishment of the current court system, and this Act has been amended from time to time since its introduction. Articles 34–37 of the Constitution, entitled the 'Courts' set out the fundamental nature of the courts system. The principal features of the system are:

(a) that justice shall be administered in courts established by law by judges appointed under the Constitution;

(b) that justice be administered in public save for special and limited cases as are prescribed by law;
(c) the establishment of a Court of First Instance (High Court) and a court of final appeal (Supreme Court);
(d) a Court of First Instance shall have full original jurisdiction to determine all matters and questions of law or fact, criminal or civil;
(e) the High Court has exclusive jurisdiction to determine the constitutional validity of any law;
(f) Courts of First Instances shall also include courts of local and limited jurisdiction (District and Circuit courts).

§2. Characteristics of Irish Law and Sources of Irish Law

17. The term 'law' is used to describe both the substantive rules of law and the legal system. The substantive laws of a jurisdiction emanate from a variety of sources, each with their own specific term that identifies them. Thus statute, common law, and constitutional law all can be described as law, but each law is very different in nature, origin, and importance.

18. Prior to the arrival of the common law in Ireland, the Brehon law system operated. This was a custom-based system that was gradually abolished by the early seventeenth century. The common law recognized and tolerated custom that was of a local or particular nature. A custom is a habitual practice, and general acquiescence of it acquires legal force. To be recognized, the custom had to be certain, reasonable, and continuous. It also had to exist in a particular locality in relation to some particular matter and other matters were governed by the common law. Most law based upon custom has been incorporated into the common law.

19. One of the bases of the Irish legal system is its common law tradition. Following the Norman Conquest of England, Ireland was the next country to be colonized, and with the colonization came the common law system. The common law is a body of laws handed down by the judiciary over the centuries and decisions from the 1700 and 1800s still have effect. The essential characteristic of the common law system is that it is made by judges, not legislators. The development of the common law depended upon a person bringing a claim in order for a decision to be made by a court that would change the law rather than the legislature providing the remedy. The common law also signifies a body of law developed by the common law courts as opposed to that of the courts of equity, which was developed by and administered by the courts of Chancery. The rules of Equity were developed to deal with the harshness of the strict application of the common law. Fundamental to the operation of the common law system is the doctrine of precedent or *stare decisis*. This doctrine states that a decision of a court shall be binding on all other courts. This ensures consistency in decision-making by the judiciary and provides legal advisers with some certainty as to what the law is. The operation of the doctrine of precedent requires there to be a hierarchy in the court system whereby an inferior court will be bound by the ruling of a superior court. Whilst courts of equal jurisdiction are not bound by each other's decisions, the usual practice is to consider such decisions as persuasive authorities and are more often followed than not. Also there must be a system of reporting decisions accurately that is also accessible. Finally, all members of the legal community must accept the binding force of precedent. When a court decides a case, the fundamental statement of law of the decision and that which binds other courts is said to be the *ratio decidendi*. Other comments of the law made by the judge that are not essential to the decision are said to be obiter dicta. Such obiter dicta may be influential in future cases where a change in the law is desirable. Where a court makes a decision the result is binding upon the parties and the matter cannot be relitigated. The matter is said to be res judicata.

20. The Dáil and Seanad are empowered to make laws of binding force in the jurisdiction. These institutions are known as the Oireachtas and Article 15(2) of the Constitution confers upon it the sole authority to make laws. The Oireachtas passes primary legislation called Statutes. It also passes secondary legislation called Statutory Instruments.

21. The Constitution was adopted by the people of Ireland in a referendum held in 1937. The Constitution provides fundamental principles of law and guarantees individual rights for citizens and is in contrast to the English system of rule that operated prior to the enactment of the Constitution. The Constitution is the primary and fundamental law of the State. Its provisions take precedence over all other inferior sources of law except European Union laws. Any laws that offend against a provision of the Constitution are invalid and of no legal effect. The Constitution established the modern democratic Irish State, its institutions, and the fundamental principles on which the State is governed. The Constitution only can be amended by the holding of a referendum and a majority of the electorate voting in favour of the amendment. Only the High Court, and Supreme Court on appeal, can interpret the Constitution and give binding decision on the rights and principles contained in it. Since the introduction of the Constitution in 1937, the case law of the Superior courts on the interoperation and effect of the Constitution has been considerable.

22. The laws of the European Community are effective in each Member State of the Union. The European Court of Justice presides over the European Union legal system. European Union law takes precedence over all national law, including the Constitution. By joining the European Union, the Republic of Ireland relinquished its sovereignty. Article 29(4)(3) of the Constitution authorized Ireland's membership in the European Union and also accepted the supremacy of European Union law in this jurisdiction.

23. International law arises from a variety of sources, such as customary international law, treaties, and international decisions of judicial bodies. For international law to have legal effect in Ireland, it must be brought into force by an Act of the Oireachtas. Article 29(3) of the Constitution acknowledges that the State accepts the generally recognized principles of international law in its relations with other states. One of the most important international Conventions that Ireland has ratified is the European Convention on the Protection of Human Rights and Fundamental Freedoms.

24. Canon law is the law of the Christian Church. It exists and operates separately from the secular law of the State and does not have legal effect, although some Canon laws are evident in the law relating to marriage.

25. The substantive law can be divided into two broad categories, public law, and private law. Public law may be defined as that which relates to the State, its agencies, or that which affects the public interest. It comprises the broad areas of constitutional law, administrative law, and criminal law. Private law relates to individual relationships in which there is no public interest. Public bodies are liable to private law. The prominent examples of private law are contract, tort, and property law.

26. Procedural law implements substantive law, and prominent examples are civil and criminal procedure and the law of evidence.

27. Regardless of whether the law is requiring a person to do something or it is conferring rights upon someone, the law can only relate to legal persons. Only legal persons have legal capacity. All natural persons are legal persons recognized by the law. Other persons recognized by the law as having legal capacity are corporations such as businesses and universities. Other bodies may be created by legislation such as health boards that have legal authority to act.

§3. Sources of Family and Succession Law

I. Family Law

28. The sources of family law effective in the jurisdiction of Ireland are of both domestic and international origin. The domestic family laws in turn consist of statues passed by the British parliament prior to 1921 and statues passed by the Oireachtas since that date. The last decade has witnessed the most expansive programme of family law reform with the enactment of modern statutes to cater for the advent of divorce. In addition, family law in Ireland is largely common law based and has been developed in other common law jurisdictions and by the Irish judiciary. The most important domestic laws relating to family law are Articles 41 and 42 of the Constitution, which specifically concern the family and education respectively. Ireland is also a signatory to many treaties and conventions concerning family law matters.

II. Succession Law

29. The law in Ireland regarding Succession is contained in the Succession Act, 1965. This Act provides for the manner in which a person may dispose of their property, both real and personal, after their death. It further provides for who may inherit from a person on their death and for the share to which a spouse, civil partner, cohabitant and children are entitled. The shares that a spouse, civil partner, cohabitant and children are entitled to depend upon whether a deceased person has made a valid and effective will.

30. There are two forms of succession dealt with by the Act, testate and intestate succession. Where a person dies, the property that they own is called their 'estate', which can then be distributed according to the wishes of the deceased as contained in the will or according to the rules of distribution provided for on intestate death. Where a person dies having made a valid and enforceable will, such a person is called a 'testator' or a 'testatrix' if female. Where a person dies having made no will or the will is invalid owing to some defect in its execution, the deceased is said to have died 'intestate'. A deceased person may also have died partly testate and partly intestate. This arises, for example, where a deceased person has a will only in relation to a portion of his estate. The remainder of the estate is distributed according to the rules on intestate succession.

31. The Act provides for a limited form of restricting the absolute right of a person to dispose of his property after his or her death. The common law in relation to succession recognized the absolute right of a testator to dispose freely of his or her property. The Roman law system, upon which the civil law systems of the countries of mainland Europe are based, imposed limitations upon the freedom to dispose of property by providing an entitlement for a surviving spouse, civil partner, cohabitant and children to a fixed share of the testator's estate. This entitlement was known as the *legitima portio* and restricted the right of the testator to disinherit his spouse and children.

32. The Roman law and common law influences are reflected in the Act whereby a surviving spouse, civil partner and cohabitant is entitled to a minimum share of at least one-third of the testator's estate. Surviving children are not entitled to a minimum fixed share of their deceased parent's estate, but they do have the right to apply to the court under section 117 of the Act for provision to be made to them where the court is satisfied that the deceased parent has failed to make proper provision for the child.

33. The justification for restricting freedom of disposing of property on death is Article 41 of the Constitution, which states that the family is a moral institution possessing inalienable and imprescriptible rights antecedent and superior to all positive law. To allow a spouse to disinherit his or her family would be at variance with this statement of principle. Further, the benefit that mothers provide to the family, which Article 41 consider to be their duty, would not be acknowledged if there was full freedom of disposing of property on death. In any event, the concept of restricting the right of a spouse to dispose of property on death was recognized by Irish law in the 'Custom of Ireland', which was abolished by the Irish Statute of Distribution, 1695 following the colonizing or 'Plantation' of Ireland by King Henry VIII. The 'Custom of Ireland' provided that a deceased estate should be divided into three parts in the case of a spouse and children whereby the spouse would receive one-third and the child or children share the other third. The third part was free to be disposed of at the deceased's wishes as indicated in the will. Where the deceased was survived by a spouse alone, then the estate was divided into two parts, to which one of the parts the spouse was entitled. The Irish Statute of Distribution, 1695 and the Intestates Estates Act, 1954 had the effect of allowing a deceased entire freedom of disposition to the extent that a spouse and child could be disinherited except where the deceased died intestate, in which case the surviving spouse was entitled to a maximum of EUR 4,000.

III. Constitution

34. Article 41 of the Constitution contains the most important legal principles relating to family law in Ireland. Article 41 specifically concerns the family and provides as follows:

41.1 The State recognises the Family as the natural primary and fundamental unit group of Society, and as a moral institution possessing inalienable and imprescriptible rights.

41.2 The State, therefore, guarantees to protect the Family in its constitution and authority as the necessary basis of social order and as indispensable to the welfare of the Nation and the State.

41.3 In particular, the State recognises by her life within the home, woman gives to the State a support without which the common good cannot be achieved.

41.4 The State shall therefore endeavour to ensure that mothers shall not be obliged by economic necessity to engage in labour to the neglect of their duties in the home.

41.5 The State pledges itself to guard with special care the institution of Marriage, on which the family is founded, and to protect it against attack. No law shall be enacted providing for the grant of dissolution of marriage.

41.6 A court designated by law may grant a dissolution of marriage where, but only where, it is satisfied that –

i. at the date of the institution of the proceedings, the spouses have lived apart from one another for a period of, or periods amounting to, at least two years during the previous three years;
ii. there is no reasonable prospect of a reconciliation between the spouses;
iii. such provision as the Court considers proper having regard to the circumstances exists or will be made for the spouses, any children of either or both of them and any other person prescribed by law, and any further conditions prescribed by law are complied with.

41.7 No person whose marriage has been dissolved under the civil law of any other State but is a subsisting valid marriage under the law for the time being in force within the jurisdiction of the Government and Parliament established by this Constitution shall be capable of contracting a valid marriage within that jurisdiction during the lifetime of the other party to the marriage so dissolved.

§4. The Courts Administering Family and Succession Law

I. Jurisdiction of the Courts

35. There are five courts in the Irish legal system relevant to family law. In order of importance and authority, they are; the Supreme Court, the Court of Appeal, the High Court, the Circuit Court, and the lowest court in the legal system, the District Court. The Supreme Court is located in the Four Courts in Dublin. The High Court is primarily located in the Four Courts in Dublin but travels on circuits where it sits in the major town or city of one of the seven circuits.

36. The Circuit Court operates on a regional basis and is divided into eight circuits. The majority of judges sit on a permanent basis in Dublin and Cork. Outside these cities, there are six circuits: the Eastern, Midland, Northern, South East, South West, and Western. Within each circuit, the court sits on specified dates in specified towns.

37. The District Court operates in a similar fashion to the Circuit Court. The District Court is divided into twenty-four districts, which are the Dublin Metropolitan District and twenty-three other districts around the country. The Dublin and Cork Districts have judges permanently assigned to them. Judges sit on specified dates in specified towns of the other districts.

38. Each court's authority to deal with family law matters, as well as other civil and indeed criminal matters, is limited by statute.

39. The jurisdiction of the various courts is divided between civil and criminal matters. The Supreme Court is the final Court of Appeal. The High Court has exclusive jurisdiction in matters concerning the constitutionality of any common law rule carried over by Article 50 of the Constitution or any legislative enactment.

40. Broadly speaking, the District Court deals with minor criminal offences that are heard by a judge alone without a jury. More serious criminal offences are heard in the Circuit Court with a jury. The High Court also can hear serious criminal matters and sits with a jury. In exceptional criminal offences, usually of a terrorist nature, the Special Criminal Court will hear a criminal prosecution. The Special Criminal Court is a three-judge court that sits without a jury and is a branch of the High Court.

41. The jurisdiction of the courts in civil matters is determined by reference to the monetary value of the action. The maximum awards the District Court and the Circuit Court can make are EUR 6,350 and EUR 38,092 respectively. The Circuit Court's jurisdiction concerning land must not exceed EUR 3,000,000 in value. The High Court has an unlimited jurisdiction in terms of the amount that it can award.

II. The High Court Family Law Jurisdiction

42. Historically, matrimonial causes and matters were solely dealt with by the Ecclesiastical Court of the Established Church. The position in Ireland was the same as in England in that these courts had exclusive jurisdiction in nullity proceedings, divorce *a mensa et thoro* (now known as judicial separation), and the now abolished actions for restitution of conjugal rights and jactitation of marriage. There was no authority to grant a decree of divorce. Parliament, however, could pass a special Act dissolving a marriage. The position only changed with the successful passing of the Fifteenth Amendment of the Constitution, which first provided for the making of legislation for the grant of a decree of divorce in the form of the Family Law (Divorce) Act, 1996. The current jurisdiction of the High Court in matrimonial matters arose through a series of legislative enactments. Section 21 of the Irish Church Act, 1869 terminated the jurisdiction of the Ecclesiastical Courts and section 13 of Matrimonial Causes and Marriages Law (Ireland) Amendment Act, 1870 vested that former jurisdiction in the Courts of Matrimonial Causes and Matters, which was established by the 1870 Act. The Judicature (Ireland) Act, 1877 in turn vested this jurisdiction in the permanent division of the Supreme Court of Judicature in Ireland, known as Her Majesty's High Court of Justice in Ireland, and was exercised by the Judge of the Probate and Matrimonial Division. On the establishment of Saorstát Éireann, the Irish Free State, the jurisdiction was conferred upon a new High Court of Justice created in turn by the Courts of Justice Act, 1924.

43. In the mid to late 1980s, certain High Court judges interpreted the conferring of this jurisdiction on the High Court in strict terms and were thus reluctant to develop the law of nullity on the novel grounds such as inability to enter into and sustain a normal marital relationship based upon a mental illness, gross immaturity, or homosexual orientation. This development of the law of nullity has, however, been endorsed by the Supreme Court but with some restriction and caution expressed.

44. There is no separate division of the High Court that deals with family law proceedings as is the case in England and Wales. Currently, a High Court judge is assigned to hear family law matters as set out below. As indicated, the High Court has jurisdiction to determine petitions for nullity as does the Circuit Court by virtue of section 38(1) of the Family Law Act, 1995. In nullity proceedings, there is no jurisdiction to grant preliminary or ancillary reliefs such as for maintenance or orders under the Domestic Violence Act.

45. The High Court exercises exclusive jurisdiction in only adoption and child abduction proceedings under the Adoption Acts, 1952–1998 and the Child Abduction and Enforcement of Custody Act, 1991 respectively. The authority to detain in these circumstances is on the basis of the State's obligation to defend and vindicate the constitutional rights of the child. The High Court has concurrent jurisdiction with the Circuit Court over wards of court.

46. The High Court exercises jurisdiction in applications for divorce and judicial separation and may grant pre-trial and ancillary reliefs in both types of applications. Other applications that the High Court can determine, either as separate proceedings or as part of preliminary or ancillary relief in either divorce or judicial separation proceedings, include disputes between spouses concerning the family home and contents under the Family Home Protection Act, 1976. This safeguards a spouse who has no legal interest in the family home from it being sold without the prior written consent of that spouse. Disputes between couples to a broken engagement also can be determined under the Family Law Act, 1981. Other applications that the High Court can hear are exemption from the age and minimum notice requirements for marriage under the Family Law Act, 1995 and declarations as to marital statuses, such as whether a foreign divorce is capable of recognition in this jurisdiction. The High Court further hears disputes as to the ownership or possession of property under the Family Law Act, 1995, orders under the Domestic Violence Act, 1996, applications for the sale of property under the Partition Acts, 1868–1876, and disputes in relation to the Succession Act, 1965.

47. Disputes arising under the Guardianship of Infants Act, 1964, which primarily involve custody and access disputes, and the Family Law (Maintenance of Spouses and Children) Act, 1976, which involves applications for financial support, may be instituted in the High Court as separate proceedings. However such applications are rare and are more appropriately brought to the District or Circuit Court. Applications under these Acts may be brought as preliminary relief applications in judicial separation or divorce proceedings. It appears that only applications under the Domestic Violence Act, 1996 may be instituted in either the District or Circuit Court. However, such applications may be brought to the High Court by way of preliminary relief applications in either judicial separation or divorce proceedings.

III. The Circuit Court Family Law Jurisdiction

48. The Circuit Court, concurrently with the High Court, exercises jurisdiction in nullity, judicial separation, divorce proceedings, and applications under the Partition Acts, 1868–1876 and the Family Law Act, 1981. In applications under the Family Home Protection Act, 1976, the Succession Act, 1965 and the Family Law Act, 1995, the Circuit Court has a jurisdiction limited according to the rateable valuation of the property at the centre of the dispute. Where the value of property exceeds EUR 3,000,000, the proceedings must be transferred to the High Court.

49. The Circuit Court exercises an unlimited original jurisdiction in applications under the Guardianship of Infants Act, 1964, the Family Law (Maintenance of Spouses and Children) Act, 1976, the Status of Children Act, 1987, and the Domestic Violence Act, 1996.

50. Provided the property of a ward of court does not exceed a valuation of EUR 3,000,000, the Circuit Court may hear such applications.

IV. The District Court Family Law Jurisdiction

51. The District Court is essentially a court of limited jurisdiction, and this is reflected in the orders that it may make in family law proceedings. It does, however, exercise an exclusive and most important jurisdiction under the Child Care Act, 1991 and the Schools Attendance Acts, 1926–1967.

52. The District Court exercises concurrent jurisdiction with the Circuit Court under the Guardianship of Infants Act, 1964 in guardianship, custody, and access disputes.

53. In proceedings for financial support under the Family Law (Maintenance of Spouses and Children) Act, 1976, the District Court may award a maximum of EUR 500 per week for a spouse, EUR 150 per week per child and a maximum lump sum of EUR 6,350. Under the Guardianship of Infants Act, 1964 a maximum sum of EUR 150 per week per child and EUR 6,350 lump sum may be ordered. Under the Domestic Violence Act, the District Court may grant a safety order for a maximum duration of five years and a barring order for a maximum of three years, which are subject to renewal, variation, and discharge.

V. Appeals and Transfer of Proceedings

54. Where an action is commenced in a court and it subsequently transpires that the action should have been instituted in a lower court or indeed in a higher court, an application may be made to remit or transfer the action to a lower court or higher court, as the case may be. This type of application is more complex in the superior courts, and the success of the application to remit depends upon a number of factors, such as the duration of the hearing and the time frame within which the case could be determined, the value of the properties and complexity of the case, and the existence of preliminary reliefs before the court from which the action is sought to be remitted. The essential test in this regard is whether the action is in the interest of justice and appears to the court to be suitable and convenient.

55. An action commenced in a particular court is also subject to appeal. From the District to the Circuit Court and from the Circuit Court to the High Court, the appeal is by way of rehearing. An appeal from the High Court to the Supreme Court only may be brought on a point of law. An appeal on a point of fact is highly unlikely, save in the most obvious of cases. The appeal in the Supreme Court is heard on the basis of the transcript of the evidence. There is no oral rehearing of the evidence. In certain circumstances, an appeal on a point of law may be brought to the High Court from the Circuit Court and to the Supreme Court from the Circuit Court.

VI. Hearing of Family Law Proceedings

56. Article 34(1) of the Constitution requires that justice shall be administered in public except in such special and limited cases as may be prescribed by law. Section 45(1) of the Courts (Supplemental Provisions) Act, 1961 provided that matrimonial causes and matters and matters relating to minors may be heard otherwise than in public. All family law cases were heard in private or *in camera*. Whether in relation to spouses or children, there were mandatory requirements for *in camera* hearings in all family law proceedings. The mandatory requirement arose from the various family law legislative enactments. *In camera* proceedings prevented the media from reporting the matter and prevented members of the public and indeed family members from being present in court at the hearing of the case, except where that family member or other individual was giving evidence. Further, the court in a case not commenced under any of the various family law enactments may direct that the action be heard in public but with a broadcasting restriction on identifying the parties involved. An example of such is where an adoption order is challenged by judicial review, the judge hearing the judicial review can direct that the parties remain anonymous and that their identities are not to be disclosed. The position has now changed with the introduction of section 40 of the Civil Liability and Courts Act, 2004. The effect of this provision is to relax the *in camera* rule in most family law proceedings. A report of the hearing may be published as may a publication of the substance of the decision in various media sources. The lifting of the restriction is subject to a mandatory requirement that the identity of the parties or, where relevant, that the identity of a child must not be revealed. The court may give directions restricting the content of any report of the proceedings in question to prevent the identity of a party concerned being identified.

57. The conduct of family law cases is required to be as informal as possible. In this regard, the judge and legal counsel do not wear wigs and gowns in court.

Part I. Persons

Chapter 1. The Status of a Person

§1. The Definition of a Person

58. All natural persons have legal capacity. Limited companies also have legal capacity once established in accordance with the Companies Acts, 1963–2014. A person for the purposes of Irish Law is someone who has reached full age or who is or who has been married.[1] No person under the age of 18 can contract a valid marriage[2] unless they have obtained an exemption from a court.[3] Persons who have not reached full age are described as a minor.[4] A foetus or the unborn is considered to have legal capacity by virtue of Article 40(30)(3) of the Constitution. Article 40(30)(3) provides: 'The State acknowledges the right to life of the unborn and, with due regard to the equal right to life of the mother, guarantees in its laws to respect, and, as far as practicable, by its laws to defend and vindicate that right.' This provision of the Constitution was relied upon *in Attorney General v. X*[5] to prevent a child from travelling to the United Kingdom to have a termination of pregnancy carried out. The right to life of the unborn could be protected by court injunction against the mother's right to travel for a termination of pregnancy. In addition, the unborn can inherit property provided they are born alive after the death of the testator who has made the bequest.

§2. Capacity

59. All legal persons, natural or artificial, have legal capacity. Historically, married women possessed no independent legal capacity and were entirely dependent upon their husbands for legal capacity. The Married Woman's Status Act, 1957 abolished the old common law rules that legally incapacitated married women.[6] Apart from minors, prisoners, persons of unsound mind, and intoxicated persons lack legal capacity.

---

1. Section 2(1) of the Age of Majority Act, 1985.
2. Section 31 of the Family Law Act, 1995.
3. Section 33(1) of the Family Law Act, 1995.
4. Section 3 of the Age of Majority Act, 1985.
5. [1992] 1 I.R. 1.
6. Section 2(1) of the Married Woman's Status Act, 1957 provides that a married woman shall: be capable of acquiring holding and disposing of any property; and be capable of contracting; and be

I. Legal Capacity of Minors

60. The term 'minor' describes any person under the age of 18. The term 'infant' no longer appears in Irish law.[7] A minor becomes of full age on the anniversary of their eighteenth birthday[8] and thereafter acquires legal personality and capacity. A minor does possess limited legal capacity whilst under the age of majority.

---

capable of rendering herself, and being rendered, liable in respect of any tort, contract, debt or obligation; and be subject to the law relating to bankruptcy and to the enforcement of judgments and orders, as if she were unmarried.

7. Section 3 of the Age of Majority Act, 1985.
8. Section 4 of the Age of Majority Act, 1985.

Chapter 2. Registration of Civil Status

§1. The Registrar

61. The Registrar-General is the person responsible for registering all births, marriages, and deaths in the Republic of Ireland. The registration of these events is governed by a number of statutes.[9] The legislation makes it a legal requirement to register all births, marriages, and deaths that occur. Records of these events are recorded locally where the event occurs and are held nationally in the General Register's Office, which is the civil repository for records relating to births, marriages, and deaths in the Republic of Ireland. On the happening of one of these events, a certificate is issued to the individuals concerned, parents in the event of a birth, couples in the event of marriage, and next of kin in the event of death. Records of births, marriages (other than Roman Catholic), and deaths date back to 1 April 1845. Records of Roman Catholic date back to 1 January 1864.

62. All certificates issued by the Registrar are conclusive proof of the facts contained therein. All certificates are legal documents of a very important nature. A birth certificate is necessary to apply for a passport for a child. A decree of divorce cannot be granted unless a certificate of marriage is produced to the court. Likewise, the estate of a deceased person cannot receive a grant of Probate or Letters of Administration without a death certificate.

63. The Registration of Births Act, 1996 provides for new rules governing the registration of a child's birth. All births must be registered within three months of the birth. The birth must be registered in the registration district in which the birth occurs. Usually the birth is registered by a member of staff in the hospital in which the birth occurs. Where the parents are married, either the father or the mother may register the child's details for a birth certificate. The forenames and surnames of the mother and father are recorded as are their occupations and addresses. Where the parents are unmarried, then only the mother's details are recorded, unless:

(a) at the joint request of the father and mother upon both parents attending the Registrar's Office personally to sign the Register; or
(b) at the mother's request upon her producing a declaration made by her as to the identity of the father and a statutory declaration by the father acknowledging his paternity; or
(c) at the father's request upon his producing a declaration made by him as to his paternity and a statutory declaration of conformation made by the mother; or

9. Births and Deaths Registration Act (Ireland), 1880; Births and Deaths Registration (Ireland) Act, 1883; Births and Deaths Registration Acts, 1883–1994; Births, Deaths and Marriages Registration Act, 1972; Legitimacy Act, 1931; Status of Children Act, 1987 and the Registration of Births Act, 1996.

(d) at the request of the mother or the father on production of a court order naming the father made in proceedings relating to the guardianship or maintenance of a child or for the recovery of supplementary welfare allowance paid for the benefit of a child.

64. Where a child is born to a married woman and a man other than her husband is the father, the father's name may be registered upon production of:

(a) a statutory declaration by the husband stating he is not the father of the child; or
(b) such statutory declaration by the mother stating that she has been living apart from her husband under a decree of judicial separation or a deed of separation for more than ten months before the birth of the child.

Chapter 3. Personality Rights

§1. Introduction

65. All natural or human persons have legal capacity to make contracts, sue, and be sued. Similarly, bodies corporate possess legal capacity and can sue and be sued, enter into binding contracts, and dispose of property. Minors, however, have limited legal capacity. To sue, a minor must have a 'next friend' act on their behalf in legal proceedings but can otherwise act in limited fashion for legal purposes.

§2. Minor Contracts

66. A minor has limited ability to enter a contract and can be divided into three main categories:[10]

(a) contracts that are binding on a minor;[11]
(b) contracts that binding on a minor unless repudiated;[12] and
(c) contracts that are deemed void under the Infants Relief Act, 1874.[13]

§3. Tort Liability and Other Causes of Action

67. A minor over the age of 7 may also be liable in tort provided the cause of action in tort does not require proof of intention and does not arise from a breach of contract.[14] A parent is not liable for torts of his child but a parent may be liable in negligence for failing to control a child or prevent a child from gaining access to dangerous materials. Thus in *Sullivan v. Creed*,[15] a parent left a loaded shotgun fully cocked that the child pointed at the plaintiff in jest before discharging the cartridge and injuring the plaintiff. The parent was held liable for failing to warn the child of the danger and for allowing the child access to a dangerous thing. Similarly in *Curley v. Mannion*,[16] the Supreme Court indicated that a parent could be liable for failing to control a child who opened a car door into the path of an oncoming cyclist.

---

10. Law Reform Commission Report on Minors (LRC 15-1985), 3.
11. These are commonly referred to as contracts for 'necessary goods' and include such matters as food and drink, clothing, board and lodging, transport, medical assistance, and legal aid.
12. A minor may repudiate any contract that contains a recurring obligation. The recognized contracts that can be repudiated are insurance contracts, contracts to subscribe for the purchase of shares, a contract to enter into a partnership, a marriage settlement, and contracts for the lease or purchase of land with continuing obligations attached to it.
13. These include contracts for the repayment of money loaned or to be loaned to a minor, for goods supplied or to be supplied to a minor, and all accounts stated with minors.
14. *O'Brien v. McNamee* [1953] IR 86. *See Nelson v. Farrell* [1955] NZLR 405 in which a minor was held liable for the tort of detinue.
15. [1904] 2 IR 317.
16. [1965] IR 543.

Liability arises here not because the defendant is the parent but because the defendant is a person who is obliged to ensure that the plaintiff is not injured by the conduct of an individual whom the defendant ought to reasonably foresee will cause injury if appropriate precautions are not taken.

68. Liability for a minor may arise for restitution arising from fraudulent misrepresentation[17] and in equity for liability to account[18] but not for fraudulent misrepresentation[19] or estoppel for fraud perpetrated by a minor.[20]

§4. Employment

69. There is a general prohibition on the employment of children under the age of 16.[21] There are, however, a number of exceptions to this general rule. Children may be employed in cultural, artistic, sporting, and advertising employment by licence granted to the employer. The child may be employed provided the employment is not harmful to the child's safety, health, or development and is not likely to interfere with attendance at school, vocational guidance, training programmes, or capacity to benefit from the institution received.[22] Children over the age of 14 may engage in thirty-five hours per week of light work outside of a school term but must have at least twenty-one days break from work.[23] During a school term, a child over the age of 15 may engage in light work for a maximum of eight hours per week.[24] A child over the age of 14 may be employed for a maximum of eight hours per week where the employment forms part of an educational programme or work experience.[25]

§5. Witness

70. No oath is necessary for children under the age of 14 giving evidence in any civil proceedings provided the court is satisfied that the child is capable of giving an intelligible account of events relevant to the proceedings.[26]

---

17. *Griffiths v. Delaney* (1938) 4 Ir. Jur. Rep 1.
18. *Stocks v. Wilson* [1913] 2 KB 235.
19. *R. Leslie Ltd v. Shiell* [1914] 3 KB 607.
20. *Levene v. Brougham* (1909) 25 TLR 265.
21. Section 3 of the Protection of Young Persons (Employment) Act, 1996.
22. Section 3(2) and (3) of the Protection of Young Persons (Employment) Act, 1996.
23. Section 3(4) of the Protection of Young Persons (Employment) Act, 1996.
24. Section 3(5) of the Protection of Young Persons (Employment) Act, 1996.
25. Section 3(6) of the Protection of Young Persons (Employment) Act, 1996.
26. Section 28(1) of the Children Act, 1997.

§6. Criminal Responsibility

71. The age of criminal responsibility of a child remains that which is provided for by the common law, which is 7 years of age. Section 52 of the Children Act, 2001 raised this to the age of 12. A child under the age of 17 cannot consent to sexual intercourse.[27] Section 3 of the Criminal Law Sexual Offences Act, 1993 makes it a criminal offence for a person to engage in buggery with a person under the age of 17. The juvenile criminal justice system has been radically overhauled by the Children Act, 2001. The Children Act, 2001 provides for early intervention at an interagency level where children are at risk. Early intervention, through the convening of a family welfare conference, can be initiated by direction of a court before whom a child is charged with a criminal offence or where the Health Service Executive is of the view that a child is in need of special care and attention.[28] The Children Act, 2001 also provides an alternative to formal charging, prosecuting, convicting, and sentencing of child offenders through the Diversion Programme.[29] The fundamental principle underlying the Diversion Programme is that it is in the interests of society that a child who has admitted responsibility for a crime that he or she be accepted into the programme.[30] The objective of the programme is to divert the child from further criminal offences by issuing caution and, if appropriate, by placing the child under the supervision of a liaison officer and convening a conference that the offending child can attend. Before a child is admitted into the Diversion Programme, the child must accept responsibility for criminal conduct and consent to the issue of a caution.[31] Any admission made by a child admitted into the Diversion Programme is inadmissible as evidence in any criminal or civil proceedings,[32] and the child cannot be prosecuted in relation to the offence to which he or she has admitted responsibility.[33] Any admission made to a conference convened for the purposes of the Diversion Programme is privileged[34] and the identity of children admitted to the programme shall not be published.[35] Sections 55–70 provide for how children are to be treated whilst in police custody. Children should be separated from adults whilst in police custody and should not be placed in a cell unless necessary.[36] Sections 58–60 deal with various notifications to be made to the child, parent, or guardian and the content of such notification. Children are not to be interviewed by the police in the absence of a parent or guardian.[37] The Children's Court has jurisdiction to hear most criminal prosecutions brought against children. The Children's Court is a court of summary jurisdiction and only where a child opts for trial by jury or where the Children's Court is of the opinion the offence is not of a

27. Section 37 of the Sex Offenders Act, 2001.
28. Sections 7–15 of the Children Act, 2001.
29. Sections 17–51 of the Children Act, 2001.
30. Section 18 of the Children Act, 2001.
31. Section 23 of the Children Act, 2001.
32. Section 48 of the Children Act, 2001.
33. Section 49 of the Children Act, 2001.
34. Section 50 of the Children Act, 2001.
35. *Ibid.*
36. Section 56 of the Children Act, 2001.
37. Section 61 of the Children Act, 2001.

minor nature or the offence is one of murder, manslaughter, or rape.[38] Section 98 of the Children Act, 2001 provides the court with a variety of punishments that may be made against a child found guilty of an offence or against his or her parent.[39] In general there is a prohibition on revealing the identity of a child appearing before the Children's Court[40] and specified individuals can attend the court hearing.[41] Sections 95–156 provide the Children's Court with a wide variety of sanctions that can be imposed upon a child convicted of an offence. Imprisonment is prohibited[42] and detention is considered a punishment of last resort. The sanctions that the Children's Court may impose include: a fine,[43] a parental supervision order,[44] a compensation order,[45] a binding over order,[46] a community sanction,[47] attendance at a day centre,[48] probation orders,[49] restriction on movement,[50] and a detention order.[51]

§7. Succession Law

72. For succession law purposes, a child can inherit on reaching the age of majority. In testate succession, a child has no right to inherit a share from a deceased parent. A surviving spouse is entitled to a minimum one-third share of the deceased spouse's estate.[52] Where there are no children born to the deceased spouse, the surviving spouse is entitled to one-half of the estate of the deceased.[53] A child who receives no share from a deceased parent may apply under section 117 of the Succession Act, 1965 for a share of the deceased parent's estate. The share a child receives under section 117 is dependent upon whether the deceased parent failed in their moral duty to make proper provision in accordance with their means. Initially the courts assessed the application by reference to a checklist of objective criteria.[54] A number of recent cases in this area adopt a subjective assessment of the applicant's position in life at the time of the testator's death and the relationship between

38. Section 75 of the Children Act, 2001.
39. Section 98 provides for the following sanctions: a conditional discharge order, an order that the child pay a fine or costs, an order that a parent or guardian be bound over, a compensation order, a parental supervision order, an order that a parent or guardian pay compensation, an order imposing a community sanction, an order that the child be detained in a detention school or detention centre, and a supervision order.
40. Section 93 of the Children Act, 2001.
41. Section 94 of the Children Act, 2001.
42. Section 156 of the Children Act, 2001.
43. Section 108 of the Children Act, 2001.
44. Section 111 of the Children Act, 2001.
45. Section 113 of the Children Act, 2001.
46. Section 114 of the Children Act, 2001.
47. Section 115 of the Children Act, 2001.
48. Section 118 of the Children Act, 2001.
49. Sections 124–126 of the Children Act, 2001.
50. Section 133 of the Children Act, 2001.
51. Section 142 of the Children Act, 2001.
52. Section 111(2) of the Succession Act, 1965.
53. Section 111(1) of the Succession Act, 1965.
54. *See FM v. TAM* (1972) Vol. 106 ILTR 82; *BC and Ch.F v. WC and TC* [1990] IR 143.

the deceased parent and the applicant.[55] Where a parent dies intestate, which is without having made a will or where a will is invalid, the surviving spouse is entitled to two-thirds of the estate with the remainder being distributed equally amongst the children of the deceased. Where there is no surviving spouse, the children divide the estate equally. Prior to 1987, a child born outside of marriage (illegitimate) was not entitled to succeed to the estate of a deceased parent who died intestate. Indeed, the legislation discriminating against non-marital children was constitutionally upheld on the basis that Article 41 of the Constitution justified treating non-marital children differently from marital children for the purposes of inheritance rights.[56] Section 4 of the Status of Children Act, 1987 essentially provided that all children should be treated equally before the law regardless of whether their parents are married or not.

§8. Crimes Against Children

73. There are numerous criminal offences created by statute to protect children from sexual crimes, assault, and neglect. Individuals who report to the relevant authority concerns about child abuse (physical, sexual, emotional, and neglect) are immune from civil proceedings under the Protections for Persons Reporting Abuse of Children Act, 1998. The government has also introduced criminal laws with extra jurisdictional effect in the form of the Sexual Offences (Jurisdiction) Act, 1996 and Child Trafficking and Pornography Act, 1998. Incest is a criminal offence under the Punishment of Incest Act, 1908, and rape and sexual assault of children are protected under the various legislative provisions. The Non-Fatal Offences against the Person Act, 1997 provides for a wide range of criminal offences for harm caused to a child. Sections 246–249 of the Children Act, 2001 modernize (respectively) the offences against children relating to: cruelty; begging, having a child in a brothel, and causing or encouraging a sexual offence upon a child.

§9. Children and Family Law Proceedings

74. A child can be an integral part of family law proceedings. The term ‘infant’ has been removed from all proceedings involving children, namely persons under the age of 18. Children for the purposes of all family law proceedings are referred to as a ‘child’[57] or a ‘dependent member of the family’.[58] A child ceases to be a child upon reaching the age of 18 or, if in full-time education, upon reaching the age of 23. In the case of a physical or mental disability to the extent that it is not reasonable for the child to provide for himself, a child is deemed to be indefinitely dependent. These age limits apply regardless of the type of family law application

55. *See EB v. SS and G.McC* [1998] 4 IR 527 and *P.McD v. MN* [1999] 4 IR 301.
56. *OB v. S* [1984] IR 316.
57. Section 2 of the Child Care Act, 1991 and s. 8 of the Children Act, 1997.
58. Section 2 of the Family Law Act, 1995 and s. 2 of the Family Law (Divorce) Act, 1996.

brought. In disputes between married parents, the governing principle is embodied in section 3 of the Guardianship of Infants Act, 1964:

> Where in any proceedings before any court the custody, guardianship or upbringing of an infant, or the administration of any property belonging to or held in trust for an infant, or the application of the income thereof, is in question, the court, in deciding that question, shall regard the welfare of the infant as the first and paramount consideration.

75. Section 2 of the Act of 1964 defines 'welfare' as including 'the religious and moral, intellectual, physical and social welfare of the infant'. Case law establishes that these different aspects of welfare should be looked at globally rather than in isolation.

76. In disputes between married parents and third parties, Article 42(1) of the Constitution guarantees respect for 'the inalienable right and duty of parents to provide according to their means, for the religious and moral, intellectual, physical and social education of their children'. The courts have interpreted 'parents' to mean 'married parents'.

77. Where there is a dispute between a married parent and a third party (e.g., a foster parent or the Health Service Executive) over the custody of the child, the courts will proceed on the presumption that the welfare of the child is to be found in the care of his parent. This presumption may be rebutted in exceptional cases, where it is shown that the parent for physical or moral reasons has failed in his or her duty towards the child, or where other 'compelling reasons' exist.[59]

78. The rights and responsibilities a parent possesses depend upon whether he or she is married. Married parents have the guaranteed rights and duties as set out above in Article 42(1) of the Constitution. Both parents have equal rights and responsibilities.[60] They are automatically joint guardians of their children.[61]

79. Where the parents are unmarried, the mother, but not the father, has a constitutionally protected status as a parent.[62] On the birth of a child outside marriage, the mother automatically becomes the sole guardian. Section 43 of the Child and Family Relationship Act 2015 confers guardianship rights on the father of a child who is not married to the mother provided he has cohabited with the mother of the child for a period of twelve months. The father may apply to the court for an order making him a guardian, giving him custody, or allowing him access to the child. The welfare of the child will be the governing consideration in such proceedings.[63]

---

59. *KC v. An Bord Uchtála* [1985] ILRM 302.
60. *Re Tilson* [1951] IR 1.
61. Section 6(1) of the Guardianship of Infants Act, 1964. *G v. An Bord Uchtála* [1980] IR 32.
62. Section 11 of the Guardianship of Infants Act, 1964, as amended by the Status of Children Act, 1987.
63. *See* particularly the Adoption Acts, 1952 and 1988.

80. A parental guardian cannot in general surrender that status. Certain rights and responsibilities, for example, custody, may be yielded or suspended, but the parent remains a guardian, liable for the support of the child, and entitled, save in exceptional circumstances, to be consulted on important questions relating to the upbringing of the child. Adoption has the effect of terminating any rights and responsibilities of the natural parent (except where the natural parent is the adopter). However, in the case of a child born within marriage who is not an orphan, adoption will be permitted, on application to the High Court, only where there is evidence that the parent has abandoned his or her constitutional rights.[64]

81. In judicial separation and divorce proceedings, a court cannot grant a decree unless it is satisfied that proper provision has been made or will be made by the court for the welfare of dependent children.[65] A dependent child is defined as any of the following individuals:

(a) a natural child of both;
(b) a child adopted under the Adoption Acts, 1964–1991;
(c) a child in relation to whom the parents are in loco parentis;
(d) a natural child, an adopted child or where one parent is in loco parentis, provided the other spouse is aware that he/she is not the parent of the child and has treated the child as a member of the family.[66]

82. The Child Care Act, 1991 as amended by the Children Act, 2001 provided for child protection measures. A child for the purposes of this legislation is a person under the age of 18.

64. Section 3(2) of the Judicial Separation and Family Law Reform Act, 1989 and s. 5(1)(c) of the Family Law (Divorce) Act, 1996.
65. Section 28 of the Guardianship of Infants Act, 1964 as amended by s. 11 of the Children Act, 1997.
66. Section 2 of the Family Law Act, 1995.

Chapter 4. Names

§1. Composition of a Name

83. Historically, most Irish parents name their children with one or more forenames more commonly referred to as Christian names. Forenames or Christian names are given to children upon their Christening. As Ireland is a country predominantly Christian in faith, most children's forenames have a religious link in keeping with the sacrament of being christened. A child is usually given at least two forenames but there may be more. In the recent past, Ireland is developing into a multicultural society and the forenames to be heard in the national schools span all faiths, creeds, and cultures. The assigning of names to children is a matter for parents and there is no restriction on what name can be given to a child. Parental autonomy stems from the provisions of Article 41 of the Constitution. A child may be called a name other than that appearing on a birth certificate, so, for example, a child named John might be referred to as Jack. This flexibility is reflected in the fact that a child's passport may bear a name other than that appearing on a birth certificate.

§2. Surname

I. Registration and Acquisition of Surname

84. Since 1 October 1997,[67] new rules were introduced governing the registration of a child's surname. Prior to this date, it was not necessary to register the surname of a child. Now, where the parents are married, the surname of the mother or the father or of both the mother and the father may be entered in the birth register. A surname other than that of the parent or parents may be entered in the register upon application by the parents to the Registrar of Births provided the Registrar is satisfied that the circumstances warrant the entry of the particular surname. It is not possible to change the surname of child once entered into the register of births.[68]

85. The following information is recorded concerning the child: date and place of birth; gender, forenames and surname/surnames of the child; forenames and surname of the mother as she was known at the time of birth; the address and occupation of the mother; forenames and surname of the father and all former forenames and surnames of the father; and the address and occupation of the father. Ordinarily, a member of staff at the hospital in which the child was born will gather the details regarding the information about the child's name registration, but parents may personally attend before the Registrar and complete the registration process.

86. Where the parents of a child are not married, then only the details of the mother are recorded in the register. The father's surname can only be recorded at

67. Registration of Births Act, 1996.
68. Registration of Births Acts, 1863–1996 and Registration of Births (Amendment) Regulations, 2002.

the initial registration of the child's surname. Once a surname has been recorded, it cannot be changed except in limited circumstances set out below. The surname of the father may be recorded in accordance with the rules set out in paragraphs 63 and 64.

87. A re-registration of a child's birth can occur in only two circumstances. First, re-registration of birth can occur under the Status of Children Act, 1987 where the parents of a child are unmarried but wish to have the father's details recorded where these details were not recorded initially. Second, re-registration of birth can occur under the Legitimacy Act, 1931 where the parents of a child marry after the birth of the child in question. Once a child's details have been registered, it is not possible to change the re-registration.

88. It is common for children born to married parents to bear the surname of the father, though some parents opt for a joint surname representing the surnames of both mother and father.

89. Upon marriage, a wife may take the surname of her husband, though this practice is not as common today with many wives choosing to retain their maiden name for professional work purposes.

90. Since 1 January 1995, it is possible to register a stillborn child regardless of whether the stillborn child was born before or after 1 January 1995.

II. Change of Name

91. As stated above, it is not possible to change the details recorded in the birth register. Changes in the register can only occur in limited circumstances and usually involve some error at the initial recording.

92. Upon reaching majority, any adult can change their name by deed poll.

§3. Forename

93. A child does not have the right to choose a forename and as seen above, this is chosen for the child by a parent. In the case of a foundling, an informant (maternity hospital staff) can provide the surname for such a child where there is no information available about the parentage of the child.[69]

94. There is no case law in the Republic of Ireland regarding disputes about children's forenames or surnames.

69. Registration of Births Act, 1996.

Chapter 5. Nationality

95. Article 2 of the Constitution confers upon every person born on the island of Ireland an entitlement and birthright to be part of the Nation. Since the passing of the twenty-seventh Amendment to the Constitution on 24 June 2004, the right to Irish citizenship for children born in Ireland has changed. The law is now contained in the Irish Nationality and Citizenship Act, 2004, which was introduced to restrict the right of children to Irish citizenship born in Ireland to non-national parents. The problem in this area partly lies with the passing of the 19th Amendment of the Constitution on 3 June 1998. That referendum gave effect to the so-called Good Friday agreement that was an attempt to bring peace and stability to Northern Ireland in the political and social spheres. The Good Friday agreement ensured that all persons born on the island of Ireland would be automatically entitled to Irish Citizenship. This was intended to appease the Nationalist community in Northern Ireland, but the phraseology was sufficiently broad enough to guarantee citizenship to any person born on the island regardless of their ancestral link to the island. In addition, the right of non-national parents of children born in Ireland to reside in the jurisdiction after the birth of the Irish born child was affected by the Supreme Court decision in *D.L. & Others and A.G. & Others v. Minister for Justice, Equality and Law Reform*,[70] in which the court held that there was no absolute right on the child's part to have his or her parents or siblings reside.

96. Irish citizenship may be acquired in the following ways.

§1. Birth

97. Any person born on the island of Ireland (including an Irish ship or aircraft)[71] before 1 January 2005 is entitled to Irish citizenship. A person born on or after 1 January 2005 is not entitled to Irish citizenship unless at the time of the person's birth either one of the person's parents was: an Irish citizen or entitled to be an Irish citizen; a British citizen; a person entitled to reside in the State or in Northern Ireland without any restriction on the period of residence and was entitled to diplomatic immunity in the State.[72]

§2. Person Born to Non-nationals Residing in the State

98. From 1 January 2005, a person born to non-national parents who have been residing in the island of Ireland during the period of four years immediately preceding the birth, who have been resident for a period of not less than three years or

70. [2003] 1 IR 1.
71. Section 13 of the Irish Nationality and Citizenship Acts, 1956–2004.
72. Section 6(1) of the Irish Nationality and Citizenship Acts, 1956–2004.

periods the aggregate of which is not less than three years are entitled to Irish citizenship subject to making a declaration of alienage.[73] Rules provide for the event of a parent's death to the extent that a person born will not be deprived of citizenship owing to the parent's death.[74]

§3. By Descent

99. A person born to a parent who is an Irish citizen or, if alive, the parent would be an Irish citizen, is entitled to Irish citizenship.[75]

§4. By Marriage and Naturalization

100. After a period of three years, an alien who marries an Irish citizen is entitled to lodge a declaration in the prescribed form, and this lodgement entitles the alien to Irish citizenship.[76] There is also provision for the naturalization of a non-national married person to an Irish citizen whereby the marriage is valid and subsisting and the spouses reside together as husband and wife for a period of three years preceding the application to be a naturalized citizen.[77] The granting of a naturalization certificate is at the absolute discretion of the Minister and he or she may waive some of the criteria stipulated in the legislation. A five-year period applies for application for naturalization.[78] Foundlings are deemed to be born of Irish parents.[79]

73. Section 6A of the Irish Nationality and Citizenship Acts, 1956–2004.
74. Section 6B of the Irish Nationality and Citizenship Acts, 1956–2004.
75. Section 7 of the Irish Nationality and Citizenship Acts, 1956–2004.
76. Section 8 of the Irish Nationality and Citizenship Acts, 1956–2004.
77. Section 15A of the Irish Nationality and Citizenship Acts, 1956–2004.
78. Section 15 of the Irish Nationality and Citizenship Acts, 1956–2004.
79. Section 10 of the Irish Nationality and Citizenship Acts, 1956–2004.

Chapter 6. Domicile and Residence

§1. Domicile

101. The common law governs domicile subject to the Domicile and Recognition of Foreign Divorces Act, 1986, which altered the rules relating to recognition of foreign divorces and certain domicile rules as of 2 October 1986. Domicile is an important factor in many family law matters. Domicile concerns the capacity to marry, the validity of a marriage, the recognition of foreign divorces, legitimacy, and succession rights. Domicile is what links a person with a particular legal system. In simple terms, the domicile of a person is said to be the country in which a person has a permanent home. It is said to comprise both the requirements of residing and intending to permanently reside. There are two fundamental aspects to domicile. First, every person must have a domicile at all times. Second, a person can have only one domicile. When the issue of domicile arises, it is a very complicated and detailed issue for resolution.

I. Domicile of Origin

102. On birth a person acquires a domicile of origin. The domicile of origin is a dependent one. In the case of a child born to married parents, the child acquires the domicile of his or her father.[80] Where a child is born and the father has died or the child is born to an unmarried mother, the child acquires the domicile of the mother. When a parent changes their domicile this has the effect of changing the child's domicile.[81] The domicile of a foundling is the country in which the child is found. In the case of separated parents, the child acquires the domicile of the mother if the child resides with the mother.[82]

II. Domicile of Choice

103. Upon reaching the age of majority and being of sound mind, a person can acquire a domicile of choice. This requires the person to leave their domicile of origin and intend to permanently reside in their domicile of choice. A person who acquires domicile of choice is said to abandon their domicile of origin. Further new domiciles of choice may be acquired. Where a domicile of choice lapses or there is uncertainty as to a person's domicile, the domicile origin revives.[83]

---

80. *Undy v. Undy* LR 1 HC 441 (1869).
81. *Spurway v. Spurway* [1894] 1 IR 385.
82. Section 4 of the Domicile and Recognition of Foreign Divorces Act, 1986.
83. *RB v. AS* [2002] 2 IR 428 and *PK v. TK* [2002] 2 IR 186.

III. Dependent Domicile

104. The Domicile and Recognition of Foreign Divorces Act, 1986 prospectively abolished the common law dependent wife's domicile rule. This rule provided that upon marriage a wife acquired the domicile of her husband whilst they remained married. As of 2 October 1986, a married woman retains her domicile of origin or choice as the case may be. The rule remained in place for marriages entered into prior to 2 October 1986. This rule was declared unconstitutional by the Supreme Court in *W v. W.*[84]

§2. Residence

105. Residence in the jurisdiction of Ireland will suffice for many family law applications such as divorce and judicial separation. The common period of residence is one year. Residence is most important for taxation purposes as this is what essentially determines whether a person is liable to pay tax.

84. [1993] 2 IR 467.

Chapter 7. Mentally Handicapped Persons

106. Persons who suffer from a mental disability are both limited in legal capacity in certain respects and at the same time afforded protection by the law. To make a valid will, the testator must attest to being of sound mind. At common law, a lunatic was considered not to have legal capacity. The Marriage of Lunatics Act, 1811 declares void any marriage entered into by a certified lunatic.[85]

107. A person who suffers from a mental illness who is incapable of understanding the nature and consequences of marriage is said to be incapable of consenting to a marriage. Any marriage entered into in this fashion is void.[86] Further, a marriage may be declared voidable where, owing to a recognized mental illness, a person is unable to enter into and sustain a normal marital relationship.[87]

108. A person of unsound mind does possess contractual capacity and may be bound by a contract unless the other party to the contract is aware the person is of unsound mind and took advantage of the infirmity. There is authority that a contract entered into by a person of unsound mind where the other party to the contract is unaware of the individual's state of mind may nonetheless be void in equity. The individual wishing to avoid contractual liability must establish that they were insane to the extent of being incapable of understanding the contract. Contracts entered into with persons of apparently sound mind will be valid provided the contract is fair and bona fide.[88]

109. In Irish law, the position is unclear regarding the mentally ill and actions in negligence or the issue of contributory negligence. The Law Reform Commission Report of 1985[89] on liability in tort for the mentally disabled recommended that in negligence actions, a mentally disabled defendant should be resolved of liability except in road traffic accidents where an objective test should be applied. Persons of unsound mind are under a disability for limitation period purposes. Thus a person of unsound mind, in general, has six years form the date on which the disability ceases within which to bring an action in tort if they were under a disability at the time the tort was committed.[90] Similarly, children who have been subjected to sexual abuse are also deemed to be under a disability for the purposes of bring an action in tort for the injury suffered from child sexual abuse.[91]

110. The Employment Equality Act, 1998 specifically identifies disability as a ground upon which an employer can be liable for discrimination in employment. Disability is broadly defined in Section 2 of the Act as including:

---

85. *Turner v. Meyers* 1908 1 Hag. Con. 414, 161 E.R. 600.
86. *ME v. AE* [1987] IR 147.
87. *RSJ v. JSJ* [1982] ILRM 263 and *D v. C* [1984] ILRM 173.
88. *Hassard v. Smith* (1872) IR 6 Eq. 429.
89. LRC 18-1985.
90. Section 48 of the Statute of Limitations Act, 1957.
91. Statute of Limitations (Amendment) Act, 2000.

(a) the total or partial absence of a person's bodily or mental functions, including the absence of a part of a person's body;
(b) the presence in the body of organisms causing, or likely to cause, chronic disease or illness;
(c) the malfunction, malformation or disfigurement of a part of a person's body;
(d) a condition or malfunction which results in a person learning differently from a person without the condition or malfunction; or
(e) a condition, illness or disease which affects a person's thought processes, perception of reality, emotions or judgment or which results in disturbed behaviour.

111. An employer is prohibited from discriminating against a person with a disability in the following areas: access to employment; conditions of employment; training or experience for or in relation to employment; promotion or regarding classification of posts.[92] The requirement to provide equal pay[93] is not extended to employees with a disability. However, an employer may lawfully provide special treatment or facilities that enable or assist that person to undertake vocational training, to take part in a selection process or to work, or that provides that person with a training or working environment suited to the disability or that otherwise assists that person in relation to vocational training or work. The equality provisions do not apply to employment in the Defence Forces, An Garda Siochana (police), or the prison service.[94]

112. The Equal Status Act, 2000 specifies that discrimination on grounds of disability is prohibited by the legislation.[95] Disability is defined in near identical terms to the definition set out in the Employment Equality Act, 1998. Section 4 of the Equal Status Act, 2000 identifies a number of areas in which discrimination against persons with a disability are affected in relation to the disposal of goods, the provision of services, disposal of any estate or interest in premises, the provision of accommodation or any related services, an educational establishment, or a club. There are detailed provisions relating to these various matters set out in the Equal Status Act, 2000 with provision for exemption in certain circumstances from the fundamental principle of non-discrimination against a person with a disability.[96] For educational purposes, an educational establishment cannot discriminate in relation to:

(a) the admission or the terms or conditions of admission of a person as a student to the establishment;
(b) the access of a student to any course, facility or benefit provided by the establishment;

---

92. Section 8 of the Employment Equality Act, 1998.
93. Section 35 of the Employment Equality Act, 1998.
94. Section 25 of the Employment Equality Act, 1998.
95. Section 3 of the Equal Status Act, 2000.
96. *See* ss 5–8 of the Equal Status Act, 2000.

(c) any other term or condition of participation in the establishment by a student; or
(d) the expulsion of a student from the establishment or any other sanction against the student.

113. A claim of discrimination in breach of the legislation is brought before the Director of Equality Investigations. Part IV of the Equal Status Act, 2000 outlines the enforcement procedure for a complainant. The Director of Equality Investigations may order compensation up to a maximum of EUR 6,350 or direct a person to take a specified course of action.[97]

114. The Education for Persons with Special Education Needs Act, 2004 also provides children suffering from a disability with the right to an education appropriate to their needs, which should be conducted, where practicable, in an inclusive fashion.[98]

115. The High Court and Circuit Court possess a wardship jurisdiction to protect those individuals incapable of looking after their own affairs. It is most often invoked where a person is of unsound mind and possesses property and most commonly whereas a plaintiff has recovered damages but has been rendered of unsound mind as a consequence of the injury suffered. The President of the High Court or the Circuit Court can make an individual a ward of court and appoint individuals to look after the affairs of the ward. The jurisdiction of the court in question often referred to as the *parens patriae*, is extended to children as well as adults. It is more common to utilize the Child Care Act, 1991 where a child is in need of protection, but in cases where a child or a minor owns property, it would be appropriate to invoke the wardship jurisdiction.

116. Persons suffering from a mental disorder may be the subject of involuntary admission to an approved centre in accordance with the Mental Health Act, 2001. Mental disorder is defined as a mental illness including: severe dementia or significant intellectual disability where because of the illness, disability, or dementia, there is a serious likelihood of the person concerned causing immediate and serious harm to himself or herself or to other persons, or because of the severity of the illness, disability, or dementia, the judgment of the person concerned is so impaired that failure to admit the person to an approved centre would be likely to lead to a serious deterioration in his or her condition or would prevent the administration of appropriate treatment that could be given only by such admission, and the reception, detention, and treatment of the person concerned in an approved centre would be likely to benefit or to alleviate the condition of that person to a material extent.

117. 'Mental illness' means a state of mind of a person that affects the person's thinking, perceiving, emotion, or judgment and that seriously impairs the mental function of the person to the extent that he or she requires care or medical treatment

97. Section 27 of the Equal Status Act, 2000.
98. Section 2 of the Education for Persons with Special Educational Needs Act, 2004.

in his or her own interest or in the interest of other persons. 'Severe dementia' means a deterioration of the brain of a person that significantly impairs the intellectual function of the person thereby affecting thought, comprehension, and memory and that includes severe psychiatric or behavioural symptoms such as physical aggression. 'Significant intellectual disability' means a state of arrested or incomplete development of the mind of a person that includes significant impairment of intelligence and social functioning and abnormally aggressive or seriously irresponsible conduct on the part of the person.[99]

118. An application must be made to involuntarily detain a person under the Mental Health Act, 2001. Those who may make the application are a spouse, provided the spouse is not living separately and apart from the spouse to be detained or is the subject of an order under the Domestic Violence Act, 1996.[100] An authorized officer or a member of the police (An Garda Siochana) may also make an application, and the authorized officer or member of the police has the power to take an individual into custody pending an application for involuntary detention.[101] Within twenty-four hours of the receipt of an application, an examination must be conducted by a registered medical practitioner. An individual can only be detained on the recommendation of the medical practitioner.[102] Where a recommendation is made to detain an individual, a consultant psychiatrist in an approved centre must examine the individual and confirm the recommendation or reject it. Once an admission order is made, it remains valid for a period of twenty-one days.[103]

99. Section 2 of the Mental Health Act, 2001.
100. Section 9 of the Mental Health Act, 2001.
101. Section 12 of the Mental Health Act, 2001.
102. Section 10 of the Mental Health Act, 2001.
103. Section 15 of the Mental Health Act, 2001.

Part II. Family Law

Chapter 1. Marriage

§1. The Nature of Marriage

119. The most recent judicial articulation on the nature of marriage was set out in *D.McC v. E.C.*[104] as follows:

> The earlier attitude was based upon the premise that marriage is a contract, which it undoubtedly is, and that it should be treated in the same way as every other contract. However, marriage is a specific and unusual form of contract which involves complex human relationships. The concept of nullity as it has been developed by the Courts is not a concept known to the ordinary law of contract. If a person enters into a contract, which the other party is unable to perform, there may still be a valid contract, and the other party may recover damages for breach of contract. However, the whole principle of nullity is based on the fact that there may be circumstances in which, although the contract was formally entered into, it was in fact totally void solely because one party was unable to perform the contract at the time it was entered into. It is the whole essence of nullity that there never was a contract of marriage, the parties were never married and no obligations arise on either side. It is not a question of breach of contract of marriage, but of its existence, which is why the person whose marriage has been declared a nullity is free to remarry.

120. There is no definition of marriage but the classic statement by Lord Penzance[105] of 'the voluntary union for life (or until dissolution) of one man and one woman to the exclusion of all others' has been accepted in Ireland in *Griffith v. Griffith*[106] and comprises the four elements of being: voluntary, for life (until death or now divorce), between one man and one woman, and monogamous.

On 22 May 2015 as a result of the Thirty-Fourth Amendment of the Constitution, the Irish public voted to make lawful same-sex marriages which was given effect to by the Marriage Act 2015.

104. Unreported High Court 6 Jul. 1998, McCracken J.
105. *Hyde v. Hyde* 1866 L.R. 1 P & D 130.
106. [1944] IR 35.

§2. THE CAPACITY TO MARRY

I. Engagement

121. The majority of couples become engaged before they go through a marriage ceremony. At common law, the exchange of promises to marry amounted to a legally binding contract to marry, the breach of which entitled the party not at fault to sue for breach of promise or contract. The Family Law Act, 1981, however, abolished this remedy but does provide a mechanism for the resolution of any property disputes between the parties to the broken engagement. The mechanism is essentially the same as that provided for in the case of judicial separation and divorce proceedings.

II. Formalities of Marriage

122. A marriage may be entered into according to the rites of a particular religion or a civil marriage ceremony may be conducted before the Registrar of Marriages. Church marriages must conform to the formalities of the particular religion. All marriages must conform with section 32 of the Family Law Act, 1995, which stipulates that a marriage will be void unless three months' notice in writing prior to the date on which the marriage is to be celebrated is given to the Registrar of Marriages of the parties' intention to marry. An application may be made to court for an exemption of this requirement.

123. The minimum civil law requirements are that the parties to the marriage exchange their mutual consents to the marriage in the presence of a priest in holy orders. All marriages celebrated in the various religions meet this minimum requirement but the various religious rites require further formalities to be satisfied as do civil marriages before the Registrar of Marriages.

A. Roman Catholic Marriages

124. These form the vast majority of marriages celebrated in Ireland and may be celebrated by Episcopal dispensation or after publication of the banns whereby both parties must be Roman Catholics. Such marriages also may be celebrated by ordinary licence on seven days' notice to the licensor who is nominated by a bishop and who forwards the notice to the officiating priest in the places of worship of the parties. The marriage is solemnized in a Roman Catholic Church with open doors and in the presence of two or more witnesses. Only one of the parties needs to be a Roman Catholic. A marriage may also be solemnized by Registrar's certificate, which requires the parties to provide details including their names and surnames, age, occupation, status, place of residence, worship, and solemnization of marriage.

B. Church of Ireland Marriages

125. Church of Ireland marriages may be celebrated by a special licence granted by any Bishop whereby either party is a Protestant Episcopalian. A certificate identical to that necessary for a Roman Catholic marriage must be forwarded to the officiating clergyman. A marriage solemnized by ordinary licence requires notice to the licensor by one of the parties who must have resided for at least seven days in the district or have been a member of the congregation for not less than three months. One of the parties must affirm that there is no lawful impediment to the marriage and that for fourteen days their place of residence has been within the district. Where the marriage is to be solemnized after publication of banns, both parties must be Protestant Episcopalians. A marriage also may be solemnized on production of a Registrar's certificate. Every marriage must be publicly solemnized in the presence of at least two witnesses and an officiating clergyman. This requirement applies to Presbyterian, other Protestant, and Jewish marriages.

C. Presbyterian Marriages

126. Such marriages may be celebrated by special licence granted by the Moderator or by ordinary licence. Only one party needs to be a Presbyterian. The requirements that govern special licences and ordinary licences for Church of Ireland marriages likewise apply for Presbyterian marriages. In the case of a marriage celebrated by publication of banns, both parties must be Presbyterians and the banns are read on three consecutive Sundays. Six days prior to the first reading of the banns, a notice containing details of the parties' names, surnames, place of worship, and abode must be given to the minister before whom the banns will be read.

D. Other Protestant Marriages

127. Such marriages may be celebrated either by special licence granted by the Moderator, Chairman, Secretary, or President as the case may be, or by Registrar's certificate or licence.

E. Jewish Marriages

128. Such marriages are celebrated either by special licence or on production of the Registrar's certificate.

F. Marriages in the Office of the Registrar

129. Such marriages are commonly known as civil marriages and require the Registrar's certificate or licence before they can be solemnized. The parties must meet minimum residence requirements within the district and a notice must be provided to the Registrar before the licence or certificate can issue. The notice states: the names and surname; profession; age; ordinary place of worship, residence, and solemnization of marriage whether by Registrar's licence or certificate. Marriage by licence requires fifteen days' residence within the district and seven days' residence in the case of a marriage by certificate. The licence to marry is issued seven days after notice and the certificate fifteen days after notice. Any person may register a *caveat* or impediment to the issuing of a licence or certificate, which the Registrar-General can investigate. No licence or certificate of marriage may issue until the caveat or impediment is removed. In case of ill health certified by a doctor, a special licence may be issued by the Registrar-General and the marriage may be solemnized at any time and in any place in the presence of two witnesses and the Registrar for the District. Marriages are solemnized in a registry office with open doors before two witnesses and the Registrar.

III. Different Sex

130. The generally accepted position, prior to the Thirty-Fourth Amendment to the Constitution, was that the parties to a valid marriage must be of the opposite sex. In *Foy v. An t-Ard Chlaraitheoir and Ors*,[107] the plaintiff was a male to female transsexual whose initial attempt to have her sex recorded at birth altered to reflect the gender reassignment surgery she had undergone failed.[108] The matter was reheard in light of the decision of the European Court of Human Rights (ECHR) in *Goodwin v. The United Kingdom*.[109] The High Court held that there was a violation of the plaintiff's right to respect family life and made a declaration that domestic Irish law was incompatible with the Convention. The Court offered no view on a violation of Article 12 as the plaintiff was not free to marry at the time the decision was delivered. The Gender Recognition Act 2015 entitles a post-operative transsexual to apply for a certificate changing the original entry of sex in the Register of Births.

IV. Consanguinity

131. The Marriage Act, 1835 renders void a marriage between a man to any of the individuals in Table A and the marriage of a woman to any of the individuals in Table B. There is no distinction between half and whole blood in this regard: These prohibited degrees of relationship equally apply to same-sex marriages:

107. [2007] IEHC 470, 19 Oct. 2007.
108. Unreported High Court, 9 Jul. 2002.
109. [2002] 35 E.H.R.R. 447.

Table A	*Table B*
A man may not marry his:	*A woman may not marry her:*
Grandmother	Grandfather
Grandfather's Wife	Grandmother's Husband
Wife's Grandmother	Husband's Grandfather
Father's Sister	Father's Brother
Mother's Sister	Mother's Brother
Father's Brother's Wife	Father's Sister's Husband
Mother's Brother's Wife	Mother's Sister's Husband
Wife's Father's Sister	Husband's Father's Brother
Wife's Mother's Sister	Husband's Mother's Brother
Mother	Father
Stepmother	Stepfather
Wife's Mother	Husband's Father
Daughter	Son
Wife's Daughter	Husband's Son
Son's Wife	Daughter's Husband
Sister	Brother
Son's Daughter	Son's Son
Daughter's Daughter	Daughter's Son
Son's Wife	Son's Daughter's Husband
Daughter's Son's Wife	Daughter's Husband
Wife's Son's Daughter	Husband's Son's Son
Wife's Daughter's Daughter	Husband's Daughter's Son
Brother's Daughter	Brother's Son
Sisters' Daughter	Sister's Son
Brother's Son's Wife	Brother's Daughter's Husband
Sister's Son's Wife	Sister's Daughter's Husband
Wife's Brother's Daughter	Husband's Brothers' Son
Wife's Sister's Daughter	Husband's Sister's Son

132. The Deceased Wife's Sister Act, 1907 entitled a man to marry his deceased wife's sister and the Deceased Husband's Brother Act, 1921 entitled a woman to marry her deceased husband's brother. The requirement here is for the termination of the former *marriage* by the death of the spouse, and thus a divorced spouse cannot marry his or her sister-in-law or brother-in-law. The 1907 Act was declared unconstitutional by the High Court in *O'Shea v. O'Shea v. Ireland and the Attorney General*[110] because it infringed the constitutional right of an individual to marry.

V. Age and Notice

133. The minimum age at which an individual may marry is 18. Section 31 of the Family Law Act, 1995 raised the age threshold from 16 years of age to the present requirement. An application to court may be made to declare the party or parties exempt from the age requirement under section 33. Section 32 of the Family Law Act, 1995 requires an intending couple to give three months' notice of the date on which they propose to marry. An order dispensing with this requirement may be obtained in accordance with section 33 of the Act. Failure to comply with these statutory requirements renders any marriage void.

VI. Prior Marriage

134. At common law a person cannot validly marry if the person is already validly married at the time of the marriage in question. A decree of nullity can retrospectively render a second marriage valid where the first marriage is declared void.[111]

VII. Monogamy

135. The common law requires that all marriages be monogamous in that a person can only be validly married to another person of the opposite sex at any one time. Polygamous marriages are void as are potentially polygamous marriages.[112] Where a party enters a second marriage whilst validly married to another, the second marriage is void and the parties are liable to prosecution for the criminal offence of bigamy. Such prosecutions are rare. Where a person is party to a void marriage for which no decree of nullity is required, that person may enter a second marriage because the first marriage is deemed never to have occurred. Likewise, a person who obtains a foreign divorce that is capable of recognition in this jurisdiction may lawfully remarry. In these circumstances, it is advisable to obtain either a decree of nullity or a declaration that the foreign divorce is capable of recognition.

VIII. Absence of Formalities

136. Failure to provide three months' notice to the Registrar of Marriages of the parties' intention to marry under section 32 of the Family Law Act, 1995 unless

110. Unreported High Court, 17 Oct. 1996, Laffoy J.
111. *KED (KC) v. MC* [1987] ILRM 187 and *B. v. R.* [1996] 3 IR 549.
112. *Conlon v. Mohammed* [1987] ILRM 172, [1989] ILRM 523.

exempted by court order. Non-observance of formalities of marriage as prescribed by the different religious beliefs and set out in the Marriages Acts, 1844–1972, which, in general, do not invalidate a marriage unless both parties knowingly and wilfully disregard certain requirements.

IX. Absence of Consent

137. A fully free exercise of the independent will of the parties is an essential requirement for a valid consent to a marriage. A marriage is void if there is no valid consent given by either of parties to the marriage. Where a consent to a marriage is given but there is proof of any one of the following factors, the consent to the marriage is said to be apparent rather than real, the effect of which renders the marriage void.

A. Mental Illness

138. As seen above, the Marriage of Lunatics Act, 1811 provides a statutory basis upon which a marriage is deemed void. Also at common law, where one of the parties can be proven to be suffering from a recognized psychiatric illness at the time when the marriage is entered into and that that illness prevents the party in question from providing a full, free, and informed consent, then the marriage is void, as no consent to enter the marriage has been given. The requirement is two-fold and cumulative. There must not only be proof of a recognized mental illness such as schizophrenia or manic depression, but there must also be proof that the illness in question is both present at the time the ceremony of marriage is conducted and that the illness prevents the giving of the necessary consent by the party in question. The basis on which a court will declare the marriage void is that the party was incapable of understanding the nature and consequences of the marriage contract. This is in essence a fundamental defect in the marriage contract that renders it null and void. Proof of a mental illness present in one of the parties does not by itself satisfy the requirement for declaring the marriage void, and to this extent, the courts have declared that parties to a marriage that did suffer from a mental illness at the time of the ceremony was entered into were capable of validly consenting to the marriage. It is very rare for a court to decide that a party was incapable of consenting to a marriage due to the presence of a mental illness, and the only recent decisions where a decree of nullity were granted on this basis are *ME v. AE*[113] and *S. v. J. (orse S).*[114] Where a court refuses a decree on the void ground of insanity, the court invariably grants a decree on the basis of the voidable ground of inability to enter into and sustain a normal marital relationship.

113. [1987] IR 147.
114. [1998] 1 *The Family Law Journal* 8.

B. *Intoxication*

139. There has been no reported case in which a decree has been granted on the basis that one of the parties was so intoxicated by alcohol or narcotics that they were incapable of validly consenting to the marriage. The ground has, however, been accepted in principle as a basis for granting a decree in *Sullivan v. Sullivan.*[115] In both *Legeyt v. O'Brien*[116] and *R. McG v. K. McG (orse N),*[117] the court did not accept that the petitioner was so intoxicated at the time of the ceremony as to be incapable of validly consenting.

C. *Duress, Intimidation, Undue Influence, and External Pressure*

140. Historically this ground was limited to the presence of a threat to the life, liberty, or limb of one of the parties to the marriage. In this regard the Irish courts followed their English counterparts in only granting a decree of nullity where the party consented to the marriage only to avoid the alternative of the threat being carried out by the other party to the marriage or by a third party. The early case law concerned false allegations of pregnancy and having committed unlawful carnal knowledge (sexual intercourse with a girl under the age of consent) by the respondent the sole purpose of which was to coerce the petitioner into marrying as in *Griffith v. Griffith*[118] and *Kelly v. Kelly.*[119] Other cases of duress concern the petitioner consenting to marriage where they have been in a relationship with the respondent that courts describe as one of *emotional bondage* to the extent that they are unable to freely consent to the marriage, as in *B. v. D.*[120] *and S. v. O'S.*[121] A threat of suicide by the respondent has also amounted to duress forcing the petitioner to marry in *CO'K v. WP*[122] and *PW v. AO'C,*[123] as well as a threat of having a pregnancy terminated in *EP v. McC.*[124]

141. In the 1980s there were a number of cases concerning premarital pregnancies and the High Court divided as to whether a decree of nullity could be granted where pressure was brought to bear on the petitioner from the respondent or from a third party. In cases where the parents of the couple forced the parties to marry owing to the pregnancy, decrees were granted as *in MK v. FMcC.*[125] The Supreme Court handed down the leading decision on duress in *N (orse K) v. K,*[126] where the

---

115. 2 Hag Con 238, 161 ER 728 (Consistory Court).
116. (1834) Milw Rep 325.
117. [1995] 3 *The Family Law Journal.*
118. [1944] IR 35.
119. Unreported High Court, February 1971.
120. Unreported High Court, June 1973.
121. Unreported High Court, November 1978.
122. [1985] IR 279.
123. [1993] 1 IR 324.
124. Unreported High Court, March 1984.
125. [1982] ILRM 277.
126. [1985] IR 733.

father of the petitioner offered her the alternatives of marriage or an abortion. The Supreme Court here adopted a subjective approach in examining the petitioner's state of mind and the nature of the consent in the surrounding circumstances of the pressure applied in holding that a consent must be full, free, and informed. This approach has been adopted in annulling marriages in the recent duress cases of *W (orse C) v. C*[127] and *AC (orse J) v. PJ.*[128] A decree was refused, however, in *BC v. LO'F (orse LC),*[129] where the court was not satisfied that, notwithstanding the threat from the respondent's father that the petitioning husband would never see his son if did not marry, the petitioner was in reality coerced into the marriage.

D. Defective Knowledge of a Material Fact

142. In *MO'M (orse O'C) v. BO'C,*[130] the Supreme Court, relying upon *N (orse K) v. K,*[131] held that the fact that the respondent, here a laicized priest, had failed to reveal to the petitioner that he had attended a psychiatrist as part of his laicizing process, was a material fact that the petitioner was entitled to be made aware of before consenting to the marriage. The petitioner swore that had she been aware of this fact, she would not have consented to the marriage with the respondent. On the basis of the petitioner's subjective and retrospective sworn testimony, the Supreme Court declared the marriage void. Similar reasoning was adopted in the High Court in *BJM v. CM,*[132] where the fact that the petitioner was unaware of his wife's physical disfigurement entitled him to a decree of nullity on the basis that he would not have consented had been aware of such disfigurement. In the Circuit Court, a decree was granted where the petitioner swore that had she known that the respondent was both an alcoholic and had a gambling addiction, she would not have married him in *MJ v. DPM.*[133] This appears to be the current ambit of the Supreme Court decision of *MO'M (orse O'C) v. BO'C* [1996] 1 IR 206, as the Supreme Court has recently refused a decree on a claim that the petitioner was unaware of his wife's pre- and post-marital relationship with another man in *PF v. GO'M (orse G.F.).*[134] In this case, the court was of the view that the Supreme Court in *MO'M (orse O'C) v. BO'C*[135] could not have intended the decision to extend to the personal characteristics of the petitioner and was limited to the psychiatric condition of the petitioner.

127. [1989] IR 696.
128. [1995] 2 IR 253.
129. Unreported High Court, November 1994.
130. [1996] 1 IR 206.
131. [1985] IR 733.
132. [1996] 2 IR 574.
133. ILT No. 8, 1998 126.
134. [2001] 3 IR 1.
135. [1996] 1 IR 206.

E. *Fraud, Mistake, and Misrepresentation*

143. Historically, according to the authority of *Swift v. Kelly*,[136] the role of mistake and misrepresentation played a restrictive role in the law of nullity. The mistake or misrepresentation to void the contract of marriage had to be in relation to the person as opposed to such matters as their lineage or wealth.[137]

144. Fraud only operated to void the marriage where the fraud procured an apparent rather than a real consent. Fraud in itself would not void the marriage, and thus the concealing of a pregnancy by another man and infidelity on the eve of the marriage would not amount to fraud, which would void the marriage.

145. More recently, however, the deliberate concealment of a homosexual orientation by the husband in *F. v. F.*[138] amounted to the wife having given an apparent rather than a true consent to the marriage. The decision in *MO'M (orse O'C) v. BO'C*[139] now, however, puts into doubt the decision in *Swift v. Kelly*,[140] whereby the failure to disclose a material fact to the other party to the marriage can void that marriage.

F. *Intention to Not Fulfil a Fundamental Term of the Marriage Contract*

146. In *S. v. S.*,[141] Kenny J. indicated *obiter* that an intention not to consummate the marriage, which was an essential feature of the marriage contract, could void the marriage. No marriage has ever been annulled on this basis and the Supreme Court in *H.S. v. J.S.*[142] rejected that an intention to obtain a foreign divorce in the event that marriage failed amounted to an intention to not fulfil a fundamental term of the marriage contract.

X. Consequences

147. Where a marriage is declared void on one of the above grounds, the marriage is deemed *void ab initio* (from its inception) to the extent that no marriage occurred. No decree need be sought but it is unadvisable to not to obtain a decree of nullity in these circumstances. There are no ancillary reliefs available upon the grant of a decree of nullity, but disputes in relation to property can be resolved under section 36 of the Family Law Act, 1995. There are constitutional law implications as the unit loses the status of a family under Article 41 of the Constitution. Where the applicant applies as a spouse, none of the protections afforded under the Family

136. (1835) Knapp 257.
137. *See* the recent case of *LB v. T. MacC*, Unreported High Court, 20 Dec. 2004, O'Higgins J.
138. [1991] 1 IR 438.
139. [1996] 1 IR 206.
140. (1835) 3 Knapp 257.
141. Unreported Supreme Court, July 1973.
142. [1992] 2 *The Family Law Journal* 33.

Home Protection Act, 1976 or the Domestic Violence Act, 1996 are available. Likewise, there is no right to see maintenance and no succession rights exist. There are complicated rules relating to the guardianship rights of fathers where a decree of nullity is granted. In the case of a void marriage, a father retains his guardianship rights in relation to his children provided that he reasonably believed that the ceremony of marriage he entered into was valid at the time. There is a presumption that fathers in these circumstances reasonably believed the marriage ceremony was valid at that time.[143]

§3. Effects of Marriage

I. Taking the Husband's Name

148. On marriage, a wife can take the surname of her husband. This occurs by way of custom or tradition and is not based in law. The practice is not as common in modern Ireland and where it does occur, the wife often retains her maiden name for professional or work purposes.

II. Consortium

149. Historically the common law viewed a wife as the property of the husband. Where the husband was deprived of the society (consortium) and services (servitium) of his wife, he could bring an action against the wrongdoer for compensation for the amount of the loss of his wife's services and any other loss incurred by the injury to his wife. Compensation could be awarded for the period for which the loss of servitium or consortium existed but not for future impairment. The wife enjoyed no similar rights.

150. In *McKinley v. The Minister for Defence*,[144] the Supreme Court indicated that these rights arise from the important position that marriage enjoys under the constitution and were conferred upon both husband and wife.

III. Sexual Intercourse

151. The actions of engaging in sexual intercourse (criminal conversation) and harbouring a husband's wife, for which a husband could bring an action against the person in question, were abolished by the Family Law Act, 1981. Formerly a man could not be prosecuted for raping his wife, but this rule was abolished by the Criminal Law (Rape) Act, 1990.

---

143. Section 9(2) of the Status of Children Act, 1987.
144. [1992] 2 IR 333.

IV. Confidences in Marriage

152. Historically, at common law a spouse was generally incompetent to give evidence in either a criminal or civil action against the other spouse. In civil actions, a spouse's incompetence to give evidence was abolished by the Evidence Amendment Act, 1853. The Criminal Evidence Act, 1992 abolished a spouse's incompetence to give evidence in a criminal prosecution of the other spouse. The spouse is compellable to give evidence for the accused but is generally not compellable to give evidence for the prosecution except in certain prosecutions involving a sexual offence in relation to or violence towards the spouse, a child of the spouse or the accused, or in relation to any person under the age of 17.

153. Any evidence that is obtained in violation of the constitutional rights of an individual is inadmissible in court. This principle has been held to apply to family law proceedings in *O.C. v. T.C.*,[145] where a wife stole documentation from her husband and sought to rely upon it in a maintenance application. Similarly, a communication to a marriage guidance counsellor by both spouses in *E.R. v. J.R.*[146] was held to be a privileged and required the express waiver of both spouses before the evidence could be admitted. Under the Family Law (Divorce) Act, 1996, a similar privilege is extended to negotiations concerning reconciliation and compromising of proceedings by the spouses.

V. Contract

154. In civil actions, it was noted the position of the wife in the law of contract and changes introduced by the Married Women's Status Act, 1957.

VI. Tort

155. At common law, a wife was incapable of suing in her own name for damages in an action for tort. She was obliged to join her husband as a party to the action in order to maintain the action. If the action succeeded, the husband could recover the damages, but if a wife was successfully sued as defendant, the husband was liable for the damages payable. There was a limited ability for a wife to bring an action in tort against her husband. It was not until 1957 that a wife could bring any action in tort against her husband.

156. Where a spouse is killed, an action may be maintained by the dependents of the deceased against the wrongdoer. A dependent is a spouse or former spouse,

145. Unreported, High Court, December 1981.
146. [1981] ILRM 125.

parent, grandparent, stepparent, child, grandchild, stepchild, brother, sister, half-brother, or half-sister of the deceased. The action may also be brought by a cohabitant where the couple lived together for a period of three years as husband and wife. Damages can be recovered for injury, mental distress, and funeral expenses.

VII. Criminal Law

157. In criminal law, owing to the sanctity of the marriage union and the need to uphold it, various common law rules precluded the bringing of prosecutions against spouses and the giving of evidence by spouses against one another.

158. Spouses can commit the criminal offence of bigamy but such prosecutions are rare. At common law a wife was presumed to have been coerced by her husband by his presence where she committed a criminal offence. The presumption is rebuttable by evidence of the wife having instigated the offence and has been as in any event abolished in *The State (DPP) v. Walsh* [1981] IR 412. The offence of conspiracy cannot be committed by spouses but they are liable for criminal prosecution for conspiring with others. It is not possible to prosecute a spouse for stealing from the other spouse whilst the spouses live together. Where a spouse steals the property of the other spouse on leaving or deserting the spouse, then a prosecution may be brought. Where a spouse assaults the other spouse, an order under the Domestic Violence Act would be the most likely recourse for the assaulted spouse, but the spouse who commits the assault may be liable to a criminal prosecution.

VIII. Duty to Maintain

159. At common law a husband was under a duty to maintain his wife. This duty is now based in statute in the Maintenance of Spouses and Children Act, 1976, and the Judicial Separation and Family Law Reform Act, 1989. The duty to maintain children is found in the above legislation as well as the Guardianship of Infants Act, 1964. The Family Law Act, 1995 and the Family Law (Divorce) Act, 1996 contain provisions on providing financial support after divorce, foreign divorce, and judicial separation.

§4. Void and Voidable Marriages

I. Void Marriages

160. The position concerning void marriages has been outlined above at §2 I–X.

II. Voidable Marriages

161. A voidable marriage is deemed a valid marriage unless declared void. Thus it is necessary to obtain a decree of nullity where the marriage is voidable. Historically the only voidable ground was impotence, but in the 1980s the High Court expanded and developed the new ground of incapacity to enter into and sustain a normal marital relationship that can arise from a number of factual bases. A party to a voidable marriage must obtain a decree of nullity during the lifetime of the other party to the marriage. Unlike a void marriage, only a party to the marriage may seek to have the marriage annulled. There are two recognized grounds upon which a marriage may be voidable.

A. *Impotence*

162. Impotence in essence amounts to either party being unable to consummate the marriage. Consummation of the marriage amounts to ordinary and complete sexual intercourse. In this regard impotence does not amount to failure to conceive. All that is required is that there be full and complete penetration. In theory the impotent party must be incapable of being cured. Originally in such cases as *S. v. S.*,[147] *McK v. McK.*,[148] and *R.M. v. M.M.*,[149] a wilful refusal to consummate the marriage was not considered as impotence where the medical evidence established that both parties were physically capable of engaging in ordinary sexual intercourse. The Superior Courts in *R. (orse W) v. W.*[150] and *E.C. (orse M) v. K.M.*,[151] however, have been receptive of developments and research into psychosexual disorders to the extent that they are willing to view a failure to consummate not as a wilful refusal but as psychological as opposed to physical impotence.

163. For a claim of impotence to succeed, the petitioner must establish that the impotence-rendering defect was present at the time of the ceremony and that the same defect is in existence at the date of the hearing of the petition. Further, it is irrelevant that the parties engaged in sexual intercourse prior to the marriage ceremony and that the impotent spouse is capable of engaging in sexual intercourse with another person of the opposite sex. Proof of impotence is usually obtained by the parties attending a medical examiner to determine their respective ability to consummate the marriage. The appointment of the medical examiner is by order of the Master of the High Court. Such an order cannot be enforced to compel attendance and examination. Where the marriage is sworn to be unconsummated, a decree still can be granted by the court inferring that one party is potent. The Court draws an inference from the other party's refusal to attend for examination in these circumstances that the non-attending party is impotent.

147. Unreported Supreme Court, July 1976.
148. [1936] IR 177.
149. (1941) 76 ILTR 165.
150. Unreported High Court, February 1980.
151. [1991] 2 IR 192.

164. A party may petition on the basis of their own impotence, but the potent spouse is in theory obliged to repudiate the marriage in order for a decree to be granted, as stated in and *E.C. (orse M) v. K.M.*[152] Repudiation has been held to occur where either party seeks a Church annulment or where the potent party forms a new relationship with another person.

B. Incapacity to Enter into and Sustain a Normal Marital Relationship

165. The rationale for this new ground as proposed in *R.S.J. v. J.S.J.*,[153] adopted in *D. v. C.*[154] and approved of by the Supreme Court in *UF (orse C) v. JC*,[155] is by analogy with the law relating to impotence. The High Court and the Supreme Court accepted that there was more to a normal martial relationship than a physical sexual relationship between the parties. A caring, considerate, emotional, and psychological bond between parties to a marriage is equally essential and necessary to a normal marital relationship as a physical bond between the parties. Where a party seeks to rely upon the incapacity ground, they must establish that the incapacity was present at the time of the marriage ceremony and that incapacity both prevents them from entering into and sustaining or maintaining the marriage relationship. Proof of both is required and a lack of either proof will deny a petitioner a decree. There are three recognized grounds for voiding a marriage: incapacity to enter and sustain a normal marital relationship, mental illness, gross immaturity, and homosexual orientation. Whilst these are the hereto established grounds, the general ground of inability continues to develop in the form of abusive childhood and alcoholism.

1. Mental Illness

166. Where a party to a marriage suffers from a mental illness at the time of the marriage ceremony and the illness prevents that party entering into and sustaining a normal marital relationship, the marriage may be annulled. In most of the cases outlined above in relation to the void ground of lack of consent owing to a mental illness, the decrees were refused on the void ground basis but granted on the voidable ground. It is worth noting that the mental illness relied upon for a decree must be a current illness as opposed to a latent illness. In *SC v. PD (orse C)*,[156] it was stressed that that the respondent wife's latent illness, which was not present at the time of the ceremony but which was triggered by her first pregnancy after the marriage, disentitled the petitioner to a decree, as the illness, whilst it did prevent the sustaining of the marital relationship, did not prevent the respondent from entering into the marriage relationship.

---

152. [1991] 2 IR 192.
153. [1982] 2 ILRM 263.
154. [1984] 4 ILRM 173.
155. [1991] 2 IR 330.
156. Unreported High Court, March 1996, McCracken J.

2. Immaturity

167. In the years immediately following the adoption of the incapacity ground for a voidable marriage, the High Court stressed that nothing short of a mental illness would be considered in the granting of a decree of nullity. The views expressed in *R.S.J. v. J.S.J.*[157] and *P.C. (orse O'B.) v. D.O'B.*[158] were confirmed to a large extent in *H.S. v. J.S.* [1992] 2 *Fam LJ* 33 by the Supreme Court, where the court accepted that immaturity would only form the basis for a decree where the immaturity was gross or abnormal and that it prevented the party from entering into and sustaining a normal marital relationship. In none of the above cases has any factual basis been provided explaining the level of immaturity suffered by the party. This in turn led the petitioner to become an alcoholic. At the time of the marriage and thereafter, the psychiatric evidence was that the husband was immature and he exhibited psychological vulnerability and dysfunction that stemmed from his childhood abuse and his dysfunctional home life.

3. Homosexual Orientation

168. In *UF (orse C.) v. JC*,[159] the Supreme Court stated that an inherent and unalterable homosexual nature may provide the basis for a decree of nullity. The requirement is, however, subject to the petitioner being unaware prior to the marriage ceremony that the respondent had a homosexual orientation. The notion of ignorance of the homosexuality mirrors the common law rule of approbation, which operates to bar a petitioner seeking a decree of nullity where they are aware of the defect in the other party and that the defect would entitle them to a decree of nullity. It is implicit in this example that a homosexual can enter into and sustain a normal marital relationship and that homosexuality in itself does not amount to a ground for a decree.

169. In a petition for nullity on the voidable incapacity ground, it is generally accepted that the incapable spouse may petition and be granted a decree without the respondent having to formally repudiate the marriage. The only bar to bringing a petition in these circumstances is where the petitioner is aware of his or her incapacity prior to the marriage and enters the marriage knowing of the incapacity.

170. It should be noted that approbation of the marriage precludes the granting of a decree of nullity. Approbation amounts to the party seeking the decree being aware at the time of the marriage ceremony that the petitioner or respondent is either impotent or suffers from one of the incapacity grounds. In addition, approbation requires knowledge of the factual basis for a decree and of the legal basis for the decree. The basis for refusing a decree is that the party seeking the decree should not be entitled to a decree owing to their conduct subsequent to being aware of their

157. [1982] ILRM 263.
158. Unreported High Court, October 1985.
159. [1991] 2 IR 330.

remedy. An excessive delay may amount to approbation of the marriage but will not necessarily preclude the grant of a decree where the petitioner can provide a reasonable explanation for the delay.

Chapter 2. Divorce, Judicial Separation, Legal Separation, Matrimonial Relief, and Foreign Judgments

§1. Divorce

I. Introduction

171. On the passing of the Constitution in 1937, Article 41(3)(2) stipulated that no law shall be enacted providing for the grant of a dissolution of marriage. This in effect amounted to a constitutional ban on the introduction of divorce legislation. A referendum on the removal of the constitutional ban on divorce was held on 26 June 1986 and was rejected by a convincing two to one majority.

172. The issue was again put to the people on 13 September 1995, and on this occasion the people voted in favour of removing the constitutional ban on divorce and authorizing Parliament to introduce legislation for divorce but subject to strict constitutional requirements. The majority in favour of the introduction of divorce was some 9,114 votes from a total poll of 1,628,570 votes.

173. The introduction of divorce was to be questioned in two cases. In *McKenna v. An Taoiseach and ors*,[160] the validity of government 'yes' campaign was declared unconstitutional in using public funds to advocate a positive result in the referendum. Such was held to amount to interfering with the democratic and constitutional process of amending the Constitution. The Supreme Court, however, did not prevent the holding of the referendum despite the government's unconstitutional conduct.

174. The validity of the referendum result was challenged in *Hanafin v. The Minister for the Environment*,[161] which delayed the passing of the result until 17 June 1996. The issue in this case was whether, in light of the unconstitutional conduct of the government in using public funds to promote a 'yes' campaign in favour of the passing of the referendum, that conduct amounted to an obstruction of or interference or other hindrance to the conduct of the referendum. The Supreme Court held that the government 'yes' campaign did fall within the meaning of 'the conduct' of the referendum but was not satisfied that the result was materially affected by the campaign.

175. Parliament subsequently passed the Family Law (Divorce) Act, 1996, which took effect on 27 February 1996 and which authorized the Circuit Court to grant decrees of divorce. The High Court was possessed with jurisdiction to grant decrees form the moment the referendum was passed. The High Court granted two decrees of divorce prior to the coming into force of the Divorce Act on the basis of

160. [1995] 2 IR 1.
161. [1996] 2 ILRM 401.

the amendment to the Constitution as passed in the referendum. The first divorce was granted on 17 January 1997 by Barron J. in *R.C. v. C.C.*[162]

II. Grounds

176. There are no-fault grounds such as adultery or desertion for the obtaining of divorce. The system for divorce is thus a no-fault one. This does not mean that a divorce is easy to obtain. The purpose of a no-fault system is to ensure that the process of divorcing is not acrimonious whereby one spouse can blame the other for the breakdown of the marriage. There are four requirements for the grant of a decree of divorce as set out in Article 41(3)(2) of the Constitution:

(a) that at the date of the institution of the proceedings, the spouses have lived apart from one another for a period of, or periods amounting to, at least two years during the previous three years. The only real substantive issue arising from this requirement is whether spouses who live in the same household can live apart. This issue has been decided in England in *Bartram v. Bartram*[163] and *Santos v. Santos*,[164] where it is possible to be living in the same house but to be considered to be living apart. The issue for the court in such a situation is whether there is any marital relationship in existence between the spouses. The High Court has recently in *M.McA v. X.McA*[165] held that spouses who live in the same household can be living apart for the purpose of satisfying the four-year period. This has been legislated for in the Family Law Act 2019. As a result of the passing of the referendum on May 24th 2019 it is proposed to shorten the period of separation from four years to two years;

(b) that there is no reasonable prospect of a reconciliation between the spouses. Where the application for divorce is not contested, this requirement does not arise. A case has not yet arisen where one spouse claims that there is a prospect of a reconciliation but the other denies such. When this scenario does arise, it is unlikely that the spouse claiming the prospect of a reconciliation will succeed in preventing the grant of a decree of divorce;

(c) such provision as the court considers proper having regard to the circumstances exists or will be made for the spouses, any children of either or both of them, and any person prescribed by law. This requirement must be read in light of the extensive powers of the court to make financial and property adjustment and transfer orders. Further, section 20 of the Family Law (Divorce) Act, 1996 requires the court to consider a number of specific factors in the making of ancillary relief orders;

(d) any further conditions prescribed by law. The Family Law (Divorce) Act, 1996 prescribes certain requirements for the applying for a decree of divorce. These are mainly procedural in effect. Section 38 of the Family Law (Divorce) Act

162. [1997] 1 ILRM 401.
163. [1949] 2 All ER 270.
164. [1972] 2 WLR 889.
165. [2000] 2 ILRM 48.

requires either party to be either resident within the jurisdiction for a period of one year immediately prior to the institution of the proceedings. The section further requires both spouses to provide to each other an 'affidavit of means' which sets out the spouses' respective financial positions in terms of both income and liabilities. Sections 6 and 7 require the solicitors for both spouses to swear that they have discussed the possibility of reconciliation, mediation of the dispute, and the effecting of a separation agreement to settle their differences. No decree of divorce can be granted without these requirements being fulfilled. Rules of court further require the spouses to swear affidavits of welfare that relate to the dependent children of the marriage.

177. Divorce proceedings, once instituted, can be either contested or uncontested. Where the grant of a divorce and the reliefs sought are agreed between the spouses, the application for the grant of a decree can be brought in a summary fashion that is expeditious and cost effective. Where the proceedings are contested, this usually involves a dispute over how the martial assets are to be divided and the level of financial support. The proceedings will be delayed and a court hearing and determination are necessary to resolve the dispute and grant the decree. The grant of a decree of divorce entitles both spouses to remarry.

178. Applications for divorce can be brought in either the High Court or the Circuit Court. In the High Court, the application is brought by way of pleadings known as a Special Summons, which is supported by a sworn affidavit setting out the applicant's claim and reliefs sought. The pleadings also must be accompanied by an affidavit of means.

179. The procedure is similar in the Circuit Court but the pleadings are known as a Family Law Civil Bill, and the applicant's claim is set out in the Civil Bill under the hearing of endorsement of claim and contains a claim for reliefs. Affidavits of means and welfare must also be sworn.

§2. Judicial Separation

I. Introduction

180. An alternative to seeking a decree of divorce as a means of resolving marital disputes is an application for a judicial separation. A judicial separation does not dissolve the marriage. The net legal effect of a decree is to remove the obligation of the spouses to cohabit. The obligation to cohabit is itself unenforceable since the introduction of the Family Law Act, 1981. A legal separation or separation agreement, which is a deed signed by both spouses and legally enforceable, can achieve the same legal net effect of a judicial separation. A legal separation or separation agreement is cost effective. However, the agreement must be very carefully drafted and should be as effective as a judicial separation in terms of the reliefs available under the legislation. The real motivation for seeking a judicial separation is for the applicant to gain access to the vast ancillary reliefs that a court can order on the grant of a decree. These reliefs are largely identical to those that the court possesses on the grant of a divorce. It should be noted that the entering into of a separation agreement prohibits either spouse from later applying for a judicial separation. The Supreme Court in *A.O'D. v. P.O'D.*[166] held that a separation agreement even without a clause expressly prohibiting the institution of further proceedings constituted a bar to seeking a judicial separation. The reasoning was that a separation agreement achieves the very same result as a judicial separation and thus there is no need to seek a judicial separation. Where a spouse is thus unhappy with the terms agreed to in a separation agreement, they must wait until they qualify for a divorce in order to obtain the appropriate reliefs available under the Family Law (Divorce) Act, 1996. The legislation governing judicial separation is the Judicial Separation and Family Law Reform Act, 1989 and the Family Law Act, 1995. The latter Act amends the former by generally providing for the same ancillary reliefs as for divorce.

181. The grounds for a judicial separation are both fault and no-fault based. In addition to specific procedural requirements, there are six grounds upon which a decree of judicial separation can be granted.

182. The procedural requirements are identical to those for a divorce whereby either spouse must be either a resident for a year prior to the issue of the proceedings or domiciled in the jurisdiction. The solicitors for both spouses must advise the spouses to consider reconciliation, mediation, and the negotiating of a separation agreement to reconcile their marital differences. Both spouses must swear affidavits of means and welfare in relation to any dependent children.

II. Grounds

183. The grounds for a judicial separation are set out in section 2(1)(a) to (f) of the 1989 Act and are as follows:

(a) adultery;
(b) that the respondent has behaved in such a way that the applicant cannot reasonably be expected to live with the respondent;
(c) that there has been desertion by the respondent of the applicant for a continuous period of at least one year immediately preceding the date of the application;
(d) that the spouses have lived apart from one another for a continuous period of at least one year immediately preceding the date of the application and the respondent consents to the decree being granted;
(e) that the spouses have lived apart from one another for a continuous period of at least three years immediately preceding the date of the application. This ground does not require the consent of the respondent. This ground was deleted by the Family Law Act 2019.

166. [1998] 1 ILRM 543.

(f) that the marriage has broken down to the extent that the court is satisfied in all the circumstances that a normal marital relationship has not existed between the spouses for a period of at least one year immediately preceding the date of the application.

184. The last of these grounds is the most common relied upon by applicants in judicial separation proceedings.

§3. Pre-trial and Ancillary Reliefs on the Grant of a Judicial Separation and Divorce

185. Once a spouse has commenced either judicial separation or divorce proceedings, either spouse may apply to court prior to the hearing of the action for interim relief orders. The court may make the following orders:

(a) Orders for the protection of a spouse or dependent child of the family under the Domestic Violence Act, 1996. There are four orders that may be made, which are: a barring order that excludes the offending spouse from a stated property, an interim barring order that is temporary in duration, a safety order that restraints behaviour, and a protection order that is an interim safety order.
(b) Orders relating to guardianship, custody, and access of the dependent children of the family under the Guardianship of Infants Act, 1964.
(c) Orders for the protection of the family home under the family Home Protection Act, 1976. This Act prevents against sale or transfer by one spouse without the other spouse's prior written consent. Where a family home is at risk of being lost to a lending institution owing to default in repayments, a spouse may apply to court and have the entire legal or beneficial interest in the family home transferred to that spouse.
(d) Orders for interim payments of maintenance for the support of a spouse and dependent children.
(e) Freezing orders that prevent a spouse disposing of any assents prior to the hearing of the action. This is an important order and is sought in emergency situations where there is a risk that an asset, either property or money, will be disposed of by the other spouse.

186. Where a judicial separation or divorce is granted, the court may make any of the following orders:

(a) Periodic payment orders for the support of a dependent spouse and child may be made. The amount payable and frequency is specified in the order. The sum payable may be ordered to be secured in the case where the paying spouse may default on the payment. In relation to a dependent spouse, the duration of the payment may be indefinite. In the case of a dependent child, the obligation to pay maintenance remains until the child is 18 years of age or 23 if the child is in full-time education. A spouse may apply at any time during their lifetime but cannot apply if they remarry.

(b) The court may also order a lump sum order for a specific amount. This also can be secured in the case of default by the paying spouse. The amount can be paid by instalment. A spouse who remarries is not entitled to apply for an order.

(c) A property adjustment order may be made in relation to any property owned by either spouse either jointly or separately. This order generally relates to the family home except in case of considerable wealth where there is more than one property owned by the spouses. The power of the court is considerable and authorizes it to make any order in relation to any property. The order may be made in favour of either spouse or for the benefit of a dependent child. A spouse who remarries may not seek an order nor can a property in which a spouse who has remarried resides be the subject of an order.

(d) The court may make orders specifically in relation to the family home. The order can either confer on one spouse a right to reside in the family home for a stated duration or may order the sale of the property and division of the proceeds in appropriate shares between the spouses. The court may attach any conditions it considers appropriate in exercising this power.

(e) In addition to the four interim orders that the court may grant at the pre-trial stage, those orders also may be made on the grant of a decree in addition to orders declaring the spouses' respective interests in any property and ordering, where appropriate, the partition and sale of the property in question.

(f) The court also may make orders for the sale of any property subject to any conditions that the court considers appropriate. Property for this purpose is very broadly interpreted. The only property that a court cannot interfere with is one where a spouse has no control over the property that arises in the case of discretionary trusts established for the benefit of one of the spouses where that spouse has no authority in relation to the distribution of the assets of the trust.

(g) A court may make a financial compensation order. This involves a spouse taking out or undertaking to continue paying instalments for a life insurance policy to financially secure a dependent spouse. A spouse who remarries may not apply for an order and where the applicant spouse dies, remarries, or there is a material change in circumstances, the original order may be varied.

(h) The court has extensive powers in relation to pension policies. The order that the court can make depends upon the type of pension of which the spouse is a member. The court may grant to a spouse any percentage of the pension to which the other spouse is entitled and direct the trustees of pension scheme to pay to the applicant spouse the amount ordered.

(i) The court has considerable powers in relation to the succession rights of spouses. The court, where it is appropriately satisfied, may extinguish the rights of both spouses in relation to each other's estate after the death of the spouses. This power, however, is subject to the right of the spouse to apply for a share from a deceased spouse's estate. The right to apply at a later stage for a share from the other spouse's estate is in turn subject to a blocking order. A blocking order prevents the spouse from applying from the other spouse's estate at a future date. Where a spouse remarries, there is no right to apply.

187. In making any of the above orders on the grant of either a judicial separation or divorce, the court is specifically obliged to consider all of the following factors. These factors relate to a dependent spouse. (As the factors for divorce are slightly different, these differences are highlighted by the italic text):

(a) The income, earning capacity, property, and other financial resources that each of the spouses concerned has or is likely to have in the foreseeable future.
(b) The financial needs, obligations, and responsibilities that each of the spouses concerned has or is likely to have in the foreseeable future (whether in the case of the remarriage of the spouse or otherwise).
(c) The standard of living enjoyed by the family concerned before the proceedings were instituted or before the spouses separated (*commenced to live apart from one another*) as the case may be.
(d) The age of each of the spouses, (*the duration of their marriage*) and the length of time during which the spouses lived together (*with one another*).
(e) Any physical or mental disability of either of the spouses.
(f) The contribution of each of the spouses has made or is likely in the foreseeable future to the welfare of the family, including any contribution made by each of them to the income, earning capacity, property and financial resources of the other spouse, and any contribution made by either of them by looking after the home or caring for the family.
(g) The effect on the earning capacity of each of the spouses of the marital responsibilities assumed by each during the period when they lived together (*with one another*) and, in particular the degree to which the future earning capacity of a spouse is impaired by reason of that spouse having relinquished or forgone the opportunity of remunerative activity in order to look after the home or care for the family.
(h) Any income or benefits to which either of the spouses is entitled by or under statute.
(i) The conduct of each of the spouses if that conduct is such that in the opinion of the court it would in all the circumstances of the case be unjust to disregard it.
(j) The accommodation needs of either of the spouses.
(k) The value to each of the spouses of any benefit (e.g., a benefit under a pension scheme), which by reason of the *decree of judicial separation/divorce* concerned, that spouse will forfeit the opportunity or possibility of acquiring.
(l) The rights of any person other than the spouses but including a person whom either spouse has remarried.
(m) The terms of any separation agreement that has been entered into by the spouses and is in force.

188. Where the court makes orders for the benefit of a dependent child, the court is obliged to consider the following factors:

(a) The financial needs of the child.
(b) The income, earning capacity, property, and other financial resources of the child.
(c) Any physical or mental disability of the child.
(d) Any income or benefits to which the child is entitled by or under statute.

(e) The manner in which the child was being and in which the spouses concerned anticipated that the child would be educated or trained.
(f) The factors that a court considers in relation to spouses at (a), (b), and (c) above.
(g) The accommodation needs of the child.
(h) To disregard the conduct of the spouses.

§4. SEPARATION AGREEMENT

189. A separation agreement entered into by spouses can achieve the same effect as a judicial separation. Historically, the Ecclesiastical Courts refused to recognize such agreements and they were held void and unenforceable. The common law first recognized the validity of such agreements in the mid-1800s. The reason for refusing to recognize such agreements was that it was considered, contrary to public policy, that spouses could lawfully enforce the obligation not to cohabit. Cohabitation by spouses was considered a fundamental term of the marriage contract. Separation agreements are a common form of marital dispute resolution and are readily enforceable. One exception to this is where a cohabiting couple agree to separate at a future date. Such agreements are void and unenforceable.

190. Separation agreements require no particular form to be legally enforceable but most are written, signed, and witnessed. Further, a separation agreement may be made a rule of court under section 8 of the family Law (Maintenance of Spouses and Children) Act, 1976, which makes the agreement more effectively enforceable. Breach of a term of the agreement amounts to contempt of court. A separation agreement may contain any clauses that the spouses wish to include. This is subject to three noteworthy points. First, a separation agreement that once entered into constitutes a bar to bringing an application for a judicial separation. Second, a clause purporting to prevent the application for maintenance (periodic payment for the financial support of a spouse or dependent child) is void. Third, any clause that is considered to be contrary to public policy is void. The terms most commonly found in a separation agreement are:

(a) Agreement to live apart. In order for an agreement to constitute a separation agreement, the agreement must contain a clause whereby the spouses agree to live separate and apart.
(b) Non-molestation clause. Such a clause provides that the spouses mutually agree not to molest, annoy, disturb, or interfere with the other.
(c) Guardianship and custody. Parents of dependent children will formalize the custody and access of the dependent children. The clause will prove which parent has physical custody of the child and the arrangement for access by the non-custodial parent. The current trend is to agree to joint custody with one parent having the physical day-to-day control of the child.
(d) Maintenance. The amount and frequency will be stated as will the division of the payment between spousal and child support. It is most important to include a variation clause in relation to the amount of maintenance payable as the courts

have held that where an agreement does not provide for variation of the maintenance payable, then the courts have no jurisdiction to interfere with the clause as agreed between the spouses. No clause relating to maintenance can prevent an application for maintenance under the Family Law (Maintenance of Spouses and Children) Act, 1976.

(e) *Dum Casta* clause. A *dum casta* clause must be expressly included in the agreement as to its terms and effect. A *dum casta* clause is designed to terminate an obligation under the agreement in the event of a spouse fulfilling one of the conditions stipulated. The conditions that trigger the termination of an obligation are usually adultery or cohabitation with a new partner.

(f) Property and succession. An agreement may provide for the distribution of the marital assets in such proportions as the spouses agree. The clause will also contain obligations to execute the necessary transfers of interests held in properties by the spouses to one another as the case may be. Under Irish law, a spouse has a statutory right to one-third of the other spouse's estate on the death of the spouse. Thus, it is usual for spouses to mutually waive their rights to succeed to the others' estate on their death, but this is not obligatory and is a matter for agreement.

(g) Life assurance and pension policies. In relation to such policies, difficulties may arise where rights are conferred by the agreement. In both judicial separation and divorce proceedings, the court may order pension and life assurance adjustment orders that authorize the trustees of the schemes to pay to the person the amount stated in the order.

(h) Income tax. Spouses can be either jointly or separately assessed for income tax purposes. Where a spouse is in receipt of maintenance, this is deemed to be income that is liable to income tax. Spouses may elect how they wish to be assessed for income tax purposes and the agreement should set this out.

(i) Medical and dental. The agreement may provide who pays for health and dental insurance cover.

(j) Indemnification. It is most common to include a mutual indemnification of the spouses whereby each spouse will be solely responsible for any debts incurred by each.

191. It should be noted that a separation agreement may be reviewed and varied by a court in divorce proceedings. Any separation agreement may be discharged upon the terms set out in the agreement or by subsequent agreement of the spouses. Where a term or condition of an agreement has been breached by one of the spouses, the spouse not at fault may seek to have the agreement enforced by way of specific performance of the agreement. The agreement is more readily enforceable where it has been made a rule of court.

§5. Other Family Law Applications

I. Maintenance for Spouses and Children

192. Apart from the financial reliefs available in applications for judicial separation and divorce, the Family Law (Maintenance of Spouses and Children) Act, 1976 provides a statutory right to apply for maintenance for a spouse and dependent child. A spouse need not be living separate and apart from the other spouse to obtain maintenance under this Act. The basis for an application for financial support is that the other spouse has failed to provide such maintenance as is proper in the circumstances. The application may only be brought by a spouse and thus a spouse to an annulled marriage or to recognized foreign divorce may not bring an application for maintenance. The amount of maintenance payable depends upon the balancing of the needs of the spouses in light of the overall resources available to them. It should be noted that any attempt to contract out of the statutory right to apply for maintenance by a spouse is void.

193. By virtue of section 5, a court may make an order for maintenance having regard to all the circumstances of the case and in particular:

(a) the income, earning capacity, property, and other financial resources of:
- the spouses and any dependent children of the family; and
- any other dependent children of which either spouse is a parent, including income or benefits to which either spouse or any such children are entitled by or under statute; and

(b) the financial and other responsibilities of:
- the spouses towards each other and towards any dependent children of the family; and
- each spouse as a parent towards any other dependent children, and the needs of any such children including the need for care and attention.

194. There are certain factors that can affect the amount of maintenance payable. Where a married couple separate, the cost of providing for two households increases and this affects the overall standard of living that the spouses can enjoy owing to the additional expense. There has been judicial acknowledgement that a mother should not be forced to work outside the home where she has care of small children, and thus her potential earning capacity in these circumstances can be ignored. In *B.L. v. M.L.*[167] the Supreme Court indicated that in light of Article 41(2) of the Constitution, which endeavours to protect the position of mothers in the home by not forcing them to work, maintenance could and must be set at a level to avoid forcing the mother to work outside the home. Further, where a husband deserts his family, the overall burden and reduction in living standards that arises from maintaining two households should not necessarily be equally born by both spouses.

167. [1992] 2 IR 77.

195. In assessing the income of the spouses, the fact that there may be considerable investments in shares, property, and money on deposit is of relevance in assessing the level of maintenance payable. In this regard the court has a wide discretion in assessing the true financial position of the spouses. A spouse will not be entitled to diminish his earning capacity by taking out unnecessary loans or investing money in low yielding investments.

196. Problems have arisen in relation to the burden and benefits from establishing a new relationship. The courts have expressly stated that no recognition will be given to a claim that a spouse has the obligation to support a new partner. The benefit from living in a new relationship has been considered and factored into the calculation of a spouse's net income. Where a partner discharges expenses that the spouse would have to otherwise pay for, the benefit from that saving is considered, in practice, in assessing maintenance. Where a child is born of an extra marital relationship, the courts accept that there is an obligation on that spouse to maintain the extra marital child.

197. The most important factor that affects the making of a maintenance order is the question of desertion. Where a spouse is in desertion, the court retains a discretion as to whether to make an order for maintenance. It is only where it would be repugnant to justice not to make an order that a court may make the order. Otherwise a spouse in desertion is not entitled to bring an application for maintenance. The Supreme Court has held in *K. v. K.*[168] that where a spouse suffers from a mental illness, that spouse is still capable of forming the necessary intention to behave in such a manner that amounts to constructive desertion, which precludes the spouse from applying for maintenance.

198. The liability of a spouse to pay maintenance for the support of a child remains until the child ceases to be dependent. Dependency ceases when the child reaches the age of 18 or 23 if the child is in full-time, third-level education. A dependent child is child of both spouses or adopted by both spouses under the Adoption Acts, 1952–1991. Further, a dependent child is a child of either spouse or adopted or in relation to whom either patent is in *loco parentis*, where the other spouse being aware that he is not the parent of the child, has treated the child as a member of the family. Where a child suffers from a mental or physical disability to the extent that it is not reasonably possible for him to maintain himself fully, then the child remains dependent.

199. An application for maintenance for the support of a child is usually brought by the custodial parent. Where a spouse is deceased, has deserted, or is living separately and apart from the other spouse, a third party may bring the application on the dependent child's behalf.

168. [1993] 1 *The Family Law Journal* 12.

200. Under the Guardianship of Infants Act, 1964 an application for maintenance may be made for a non-marital child by the mother of the child. The dependency rules for marital children apply to non-marital children.

II. Enforcement

201. There are a number of ways in which orders for maintenance may be enforced both domestically and internationally. In the case of enforcing an order for maintenance within the jurisdiction, such may be effected by:

(a) An order for the attachment of earnings, which obliges the employer of the debtor spouse to deduct the amount of maintenance payable and pay this sum to the clerk of the District Court. The obtaining of an attachment of earnings order is subject to the debtor spouse being in receipt of earnings. In this regard, a self-employed spouse cannot be the subject of an attachment of earnings order as they are not in receipt of earnings. The debtor spouse also must be given the opportunity to state whether they are prepared to pay the amount of the maintenance order.
(b) A secured payments order may be made under section 41 of the Family Law Act, 1995 where any maintenance order is made.
(c) The Enforcement of Court Orders Act, 1940, provides that a defaulting debtor spouse may be the subject to distraint (the seizure and sale of assets) or imprisonment for the failure to pay the sum due under the order.
(d) A motion for attachment and committal may be issued against the defaulting debtor spouse. The motion can issue because the debtor spouse is in contempt of court for failing to adhere to the order of the court.

202. It is not uncommon for separated spouses to live in separate jurisdictions and thus the enforcement of maintenance orders can be difficult. Ireland is a party to a number of International Conventions, the object of which is to enforce orders of foreign courts. The Maintenance Orders Act, 1974 is a reciprocal agreement between the United Kingdom and the Republic of Ireland that recognizes and enforces maintenance orders of the courts of both jurisdictions. An order will only be refused recognition and enforcement where:

(a) it is contrary to public policy;
(b) made in default of appearance at the hearing by the debtor where the proceedings were improperly served;
(c) where the order is irreconcilable with a judgment given in a dispute between the parties in the State.

203. The Jurisdiction of Courts and Enforcement of Judgments Acts, 1988 and 1993 give effect to the European Union Conventions (Brussels and Laguno) on Jurisdiction and Enforcement of civil and commercial judgments. The effect of these Acts is to recognize and enforce maintenance orders made in the reciprocating states. In addition, the Brussels Convention may use to initiate an application for maintenance in this jurisdiction and that is enforceable in the jurisdiction in which the debtor as the European Court of Justice held in the *F. v. L.*,[169] in which an unmarried mother resident in Ireland successfully instituted an application for maintenance in Ireland that she enforced against the father, who was resident and domiciled in Belgium.

204. The Maintenance Act, 1994 gives effect to both the 1990 Rome Convention between EU Member States on the Simplification of Procedures for the Recovery of Maintenance Payments and the 1956 New York Convention between Member States of the United Nations on the Recovery Abroad of Maintenance. The Rome Convention provides for the enforcement of a maintenance order through the Central Authority in the jurisdiction in which the applicant is resident. The Rome Convention provides for the initiation of maintenance proceedings through the Central Authority of the jurisdiction where the applicant resides. The application is then transferred to the Central Authority of the jurisdiction in which the debtor resides. Council Regulation (EC) 44/2001 provides for the recognition and enforcement of maintenance orders within the EU.

III. Social Welfare Payments

205. The system of providing financial support by the State for deserted wives, husbands, and single parents has undergone change from 1985 to the present. The following is a broad overview of the current position.

206. The Social Welfare Act, 1996 provides for the making of a 'one parent family payment' to a 'qualifying parent' with whom a 'qualified child' normally resides. A 'qualifying parent' can be a widow, widower, divorced spouse, separated spouse, or an unmarried person who has one 'qualifying child' residing with him or her. A parent is a 'separated spouse' if:

(a) the parent is not being maintained by his or her spouse or is being maintained at a rate less than the weekly rate of the one parent family payment;
(b) the parent has lived apart from his or her spouse for a continuous period of three months immediately preceding the date of the claim for the payment and continues to live apart;
(c) the parent makes and continues to make appropriate efforts to obtain maintenance from a liable relative.

207. A parent is an unmarried parent if he or she is unmarried and is the parent of a qualified child and makes reasonable efforts to obtain maintenance from a liable relative. A child is considered to be normally residing if the child is resident with

169. Case 295/95.

the parent and that parent has the main care and charge of the child. A child ceases to be a qualified child when he or she reaches the age of 18 or 23 if in full-time, third-level education.

208. Where an applicant cohabits with another person as husband and wife, no application may be made until the cohabitation ceases.

IV. Succession Rights

209. Married couples enjoy a statutory right to inherit from one another. The Succession Act, 1965 governs the rights that spouses enjoy on the death of the other spouse. Prior to the enactment of the 1965 Act, a spouse had complete freedom of disposition and could disinherit a spouse and dependent children. The Succession Act, 1965 strikes a balance between allowing the testator the freedom to dispose of his or her property according to their wishes whilst at the same time ensuring that the spouse is entitled to a statutory minimum share of the testator's estate. The law in relation to succession will be more fully described later. The following is a general description of the rights of married couples and children.

210. Testate and intestate succession are the two means by which a person can inherit from a deceased person. Testate succession arises where the person who has died has previously made a valid and enforceable will. Where a spouse makes a will, the surviving spouse is entitled to one-half of the deceased spouse's estate where there are no children of the marriage and to one-third of the estate where there are children. The statutory right of the surviving spouse is the minimum that may be inherited and is known as the 'legal right share'. The testator may bequeath more than the statutory minimum, but this share must be expressly stated to be in addition to the surviving spouse's legal right share. The legal right share takes priority over all other bequests in the will.

211. Children have no 'legal right share' to the estate of their deceased parent. Further, a parent is not obliged to provide for a child after the parent's death by specifically providing for the child in a will. The only recourse that children have where a parent dies testate is to apply under section 117 of the Succession Act, 1965 where the court is of the opinion that the parent has failed in his moral duty to make proper provision for the child in accordance with his means. If the court does make an order providing for a child under section 117, the order made cannot affect the legal right share of the surviving spouse.

212. Intestate succession occurs where a person dies and makes no will or where a will is made but is invalid due to some defect in the making of the will or uncertainty as to its terms. Where an intestate dies leaving only a spouse and no children, then the surviving spouse inherits the deceased's entire estate. Where the intestate dies and is survived by a spouse and children, the spouse inherits two-thirds of the estate and the remainder is distributed equally amongst the children. Where an intestate dies and is survived only by children, the children inherit the entire estate, which is divided equally amongst them.

213. Where a person makes a will and subsequently marries, section 85(1) of the Succession Act, 1965 declares that the will is invalid unless it is specifically made in contemplation of the marriage. The succession rights of a spouse may be waived or renounced in writing by a spouse during the lifetime of the other spouse. Parties to an intended marriage may waive their succession rights in an ante nuptial agreement.

214. On the grant of a decree of divorce or judicial separation, a court may extinguish the succession rights of the spouses and preclude them from applying for a share on the death of the other spouse. A decree of divorce terminates the status of spouse and likewise a spouse's succession rights. Where a decree of nullity has been granted to the parties to a marriage, their succession rights are likewise extinguished.

V. Spousal Protection

215. The Domestic Violence Act, 1996 provides protection against domestic violence for a spouse, unmarried couples, and other relationships. The Domestic Violence Act 2018 has made significant changes to the domestic violence laws. It introduces an emergency barring order application without the proprietary interest bar that applies to interim barring and barring orders which prevented an application where the respondent has an equal or greater propriety interest in the property from which the respondent is to be excluded. Section 5 lists a number of factors the court must regard in any application including such matters as a history of violence, convictions for theft and offences involving violence, animal cruelty and substance abuse. The requirement to be living for a minimum period of time for barring and safety orders where the parties are not married has been removed and replaced with the concept of living in an intimate relationship. Section 24 enables special sittings of courts to be help outside of normal hours as well as the use of electronic medial to give evidence (Section 25). A new offence of coercive control has been created by Section 39.

216. There are five types of order that a court may make:

(a) A barring order, which directs the respondent to leave the place specified in the order and not to return. The court excludes the respondent from the property where it is satisfied that the safety or welfare of the applicant or dependent child so requires. The maximum duration of a barring order granted in the District Court is three years and indefinite where the order is made by the Circuit Court.
(b) An interim barring order may be applied for in an emergency situation. The ground upon which an order may be granted is that there is an immediate risk of significant harm to the applicant or dependent child and that the granting of

a protection order would not provide sufficient protection. An interim barring order has the same effect as a barring order but only remains in force until the hearing of a barring order.

(c) An emergency barring order which has the same effect as a barring order but only remains valid for eight working days and can only be granted once in a calendar month.

(d) A safety order may be obtained for an applicant or dependent child where the safety or welfare so requires it. The effect of a safety order is to restrain the respondent from using or threatening to use violence, molesting, or placing in fear the applicant or dependent child. The maximum duration of a District Court order is five years and the Circuit Court has unlimited jurisdiction in this regard.

(e) The final order a court may make is a protection order, which is in effect a temporary safety order that remains in force until a barring or safety order application is heard. The basis for the granting of the order is that the safety or welfare of the applicant or dependent child so requires it.

217. A wide variety of persons may apply for these orders. All current and former spouses may apply, even in the case where a spouse is a party to an annulled marriage. Further, all dependent children of current or former marriages may obtain an order where the parent applies on their behalf. If a parent fails to seek an order, a health board, which is a statutory body invested with powers and duties under the Act, may apply on behalf of the child or the parent who requires an order where the other spouse has prevented an application being brought by intimidation or threats.

218. Keating v. Crowley & AG[170] declared section 4(3) of the Domestic Violence Act, 1996 unconstitutional because an application for an *ex parte* interim barring order obtained in the District Court did not provide a minimum period of time for which the order would remain valid. The effect of the procedural rules is to prevent a respondent from challenging the validity of the order obtained. The same application in the Circuit Court was governed by rules of court making the interim order obtained *ex parte* valid for only eight days. As a consequence, the Domestic Violence (Amendment) Act, 2002 now provides for an *ex parte* application procedure for an interim barring order in identical terms to that of the Circuit Court procedure.

§6. Recognition of Judgments in Foreign Matrimonial Proceedings

I. Polygamous and Monogamous Marriages

219. The law in relation to polygamous marriages is complex and uncertain in Irish conflicts of laws. Only monogamous marriages may be validly entered into in Ireland. The *lex loci celebrationis* determines the nature and incidents of marriage,

170. [2002] 2 IR 744.

and in light of these, an Irish court must determine whether a marriage is polygamous or monogamous. Thus, if an Irish domiciled man or woman enters into a polygamous form of marriage in Pakistan, the marriage is polygamous. If a Pakistan domiciled man or woman enters into a marriage in Ireland, such is a monogamous marriage. In this regard, the fact that a polygamous marriage is valid under the *lex loci celebrationis* does not mean that the marriage is valid under Irish law. If either of the parties to the marriage does not have the capacity under his or her *lex domicilii* to contract a polygamous marriage, then the marriage will not be valid under Irish law.

220. A polygamous marriage, once entered into, remains polygamous. There is no certainty in Irish law on the issues of whether polygamous marriages may be transformed by certain events to monogamous marriages or whether an initially monogamous marriage may be transformed to a polygamous marriage. The only certainty in Irish conflicts law is that parties to polygamous marriages may not seek matrimonial reliefs in Irish courts. The position regarding maintenance entitlements and succession rights in polygamous marriages is uncertain owing to the absence of court decisions on these issues. Children born of polygamous marriages are entitled to succeed to the estates of their deceased parents. The answer to these issues depends on the courts' attitude to social policy and on what stance should be adopted in relation to public policy.

II. Marriage Validity

221. There are two aspects to a valid marriage: formalities of marriage and the essentials of marriage. Formalities of marriage concern the time and place at that a marriage may be celebrated, the number of witnesses, and the minimum period of notice. The essentials of marriage concern the mental capacity to contract a marriage and such matters as duress. Difficulties arise where the court has to determine whether a particular aspect of marriage, such as where the consent of a parent is necessary to contract a valid marriage, is matter of formalities or of essentials of marriage.

222. It is generally accepted that the *lex loci celebrationis* determines the formal validity of marriage. Thus if a marriage is valid according to the *lex loci celebrationis*, then it is considered to be valid everywhere in the world even though it may not be valid in the country of the parties' domicile. A court has to determine in what country the *lex loci celebrationis* is. Difficulties arise where the marriage is celebrated by *correspondence* in determining the *lex loci celebrationis*. Where the marriage is one by *proxy*, that is, where the parties are not present and give their consent by an agent, the *lex loci celebrationis* is the country where the proxy participates. Marriages by *habit and repute* also create difficulties in determining the *lex loci celebrationis*.

223. Time is also an important factor in determining the *lex loci celebrationis*. This may be simply established by reference to the date on which the marriage is contracted. However, this is complicated, because the county in which the marriage is contracted enacts retrospective legislation, which validates invalidly contracted marriages. In this regard, Ireland introduced the Marriages Act, 1972 to validate marriages entered into by Irish citizens in Lourdes, which was common in the 1950s. These were religious ceremonies of marriage that were invalid according to French law, which only recognized civil marriages as valid.

224. Exceptions to the *lex loci celebrationis* arise where the marriage is a common law marriage, that is, where it has been entered into but in the presence of an Episcopalian ordained priest. This exception arose from the British settlers contracting marriages in British colonial territories such as Australia. The rationale for this exception was the absence of established churches in the new territories and thus the impossibility of contracting a marriage in the presence of an Episcopalian ordained priest. The other exception to this rule is the Foreign Marriages Act, 1892, which applied in Ireland prior to the coming into being of Saorstát Éireann in 1922. The Act authorized ambassadors and other consular officials to conduct marriage ceremonies.

225. In relation to the essentials of the marriage contract or the capacity to marry, this is determined according to the ante nuptial domicile or the *lex domicilii*. There are a number of exceptions to this general rule:

(a) The rule in *Sottomayor v. De Barros*[171] (No. 2) 5 P.D. 94 (1879) provides that where a marriage is celebrated within Britain where one of the spouses is domiciled, the marriage will be valid despite the other spouse not having the capacity to marry under the law of his or her domicile.
(b) Where the marriage is valid according to the personal law of the spouses but void according to the *lex loci celebrationis* and the *lex loci celebrationis* is foreign law, then Irish law should disregard the disability under the *lex loci celebrationis* and accept the marriage as valid. If, however, the *lex loci celebrationis* is also the *lex fori* and the marriage is void according to the *lex loci celebrationis* but valid according to the personal law of the spouses, then Irish law should uphold the marriage as invalid.
(c) Capacity to marry after the grant of a divorce causes problems in this jurisdiction. At common law the capacity to marry after a divorce is determined according to the ante nuptial domicile. Thus, if a man and a woman are domiciled in Ireland and they obtain a divorce in England and the man immediately remarries there, (as the divorce is not capable of recognition in Ireland), the second marriage is not recognized as valid because the man, according to his ante nuptial domicile, was not capable of contracting a valid marriage at the time he entered into the second marriage. If, however, the man changes his domicile and marries in that country of new domicile subsequent to obtaining a foreign divorce, at common law, it is suggested that the second marriage should be recognized as valid, even if the divorce is not capable of recognition. This common law position is complicated by Article 41(3)(3) of the Constitution, which

171. (No. 2) 5 P.D. 94 (1879).

provides for the circumstances in which a foreign divorce is capable of recognition in this jurisdiction. All of the decisions on the effect of Article 41(3)(3) concern whether a foreign divorce is capable of recognition. There is little judicial comment on whether a person has the capacity to contract a second valid marriage after the grant of foreign divorce, which is incapable of recognition in this jurisdiction. Article 41(3)(3) is certain on the validity of the second marriage subsequent to a foreign divorce which is incapable of recognition in this jurisdiction; no second marriage may be validly contracted in this jurisdiction in these circumstances. This does not mean that the second marriage is invalid in a foreign jurisdiction.

(d) Irish courts will not give effect to a capacity or incapacity under the law of a party's ante nuptial domicile if the effect of such would be contrary to Irish public policy, for example where such would recognize as valid marriages between persons of the same sex or marriages between siblings.

226. Where the consent of a party to a marriage is in issue, the appropriate law to determine this is the law of the party's domicile.

III. Nullity of Marriage

227. Section 39 of the Family Law Act, 1995 provides that a court may grant a decree of nullity where either or both of the spouses are domiciled in this jurisdiction on the date on which the proceedings are instituted. Where either spouse has been ordinarily resident for a period in excess of one year prior to the institution of the proceedings. Where either of the spouses dies prior to the institution of proceedings, the court has jurisdiction to grant a decree of nullity if the deceased spouse was at the time of his or her death domiciled or had been ordinarily resident in Ireland for period of one year prior to his or her death. These rules apply regardless of whether the decree of nullity is based upon the void or voidable grounds.

IV. Recognition of Foreign Nullity Decrees

228. Where both spouses are domiciled in the jurisdiction granting the decree of nullity, it would appear at common law that an Irish court would recognize the decree as valid in Irish law. There is no Irish authority in relation to the domicile of one of the spouses enabling an Irish court to recognize the foreign decree of nullity. Under English law, the courts there have refused to recognize a decree of nullity of a foreign court where only one of the spouses was domiciled in the foreign country. There is English authority that supports the recognition of a foreign decree of nullity not granted in the country of the spouses' country of common domicile but nonetheless recognized as valid in that country. Recognition is also presumed to be given to a decree of nullity that is recognized as valid in the country of domicile of one of the spouses but not the other.

229. Residence in a country at the time of the institution of the proceedings for a decree nullity of either or both the spouses would not appear to be acceptable to an Irish court as recognizing the validity of the foreign decree of nullity. This assumption is based upon the current position in relation to the recognition of foreign divorces that insists upon the domicile of either or both the spouses to recognize a foreign divorce as valid in Irish law. Thus it would be unlikely that an Irish court would accept other connecting factors accepted in England such as habitual residence, the 'real and substantial connection' test and the reciprocity test.

230. An Irish court may refuse to recognize a foreign nullity decree where:

(a) recognition would be contrary to justice or public policy;
(b) the decree was obtained by fraud;
(c) the foreign decree offends against rules of natural justice;
(d) the validity of the marriage is res judicata in that an Irish court has previously upheld the marriage as valid;
(e) the decree is granted by way of extra-judicial decision.

231. If a foreign decree of nullity is recognized in this jurisdiction but the effect of the decree in Irish law differs from the effect in law of the foreign jurisdiction, a problem would arise for the Irish court in what effect the decree should have under Irish law. This would arise where Irish law would consider the marriage void, whereas the foreign law considers the marriage voidable. English authority suggests that the foreign law effect should be recognized and given effect to in this jurisdiction.

232. Once a foreign decree of nullity is recognized in this jurisdiction, the parties to the decree are capable of validly remarrying. Difficulties arise where the decree of nullity is recognized as valid here but invalid according to the law of the domicile of the parties as to whether the parties are free to remarry in this jurisdiction. The law of domicile should prevail, but there is English authority that provides that a marriage contracted in the jurisdiction recognizing the nullity decree as valid likewise has the effect of recognizing the marriage as valid.

233. Where the foreign nullity decree is not recognized in Irish law, the parties to the decree cannot contract a valid marriage in Ireland. If the remarriage is valid according to the law of the party's domicile, there is authority in Canada that the capacity rule should prevail over the recognition rule.

234. Under the Family Law Act, 1995 there is only provision to grant financial relief on foot for a foreign judicial separation or divorce. There is no provision to grant financial relief on foot of a foreign decree of nullity.

V. Recognition of Foreign Divorces

235. Historically Article 41(3)(3) was viewed as prohibiting the recognition of foreign divorces in this jurisdiction that in turn prohibited the parties to the foreign divorce from remarrying in this jurisdiction. The law up until 2 October 1986 was simple and uncomplicated. A foreign divorce would be recognized only where both spouses were domiciled in the jurisdiction granting the decree of divorce. After 2 October 1986, the Domicile and Recognition of foreign Divorces Act, 1986 came into effect. The Act changes the common law rules whereby any foreign divorce granted prior to the introduction of the Act was recognized if both spouses were domiciled in the jurisdiction granting the decree of divorce. After the introduction of the Act, a foreign divorce is capable of recognition on the basis of either of the spouses' domicile in the jurisdiction granting the divorce. The operation of these rules was based upon the assumption that the domicile of dependency of a married woman was constitutionally valid prior to the introduction of the Act. The Act abolished the married woman's dependent domicile rule after the commencement of the Act, whereby all married women retained their domicile of origin upon marrying. The married woman's dependent domicile rule, which remained in effect prior to the commencement of the Act, was declared unconstitutional by the Supreme Court in *W. v. W.*[172] The Supreme Court also changed the recognition rules to afford recognition to a foreign divorce granted prior to the introduction of the Act where either of the spouses was domiciled in the jurisdiction granting the foreign divorce.

236. Recently the High Court in *G.McG v. D.W.*[173] was willing to recognize the validity of a foreign divorce granted on the basis of the residence of the spouses in the foreign jurisdiction when the divorce proceedings were instituted. The Attorney General unsuccessfully applied to be joined in these proceedings to challenge the authority of the High Court to alter the recognition rules in relation to foreign divorces. The High court decision remains good law for the moment until the Attorney General is joined in a similar case to challenge the validity of this decision. In *M.E.C. v. J.A.C. & J.D.C. v. J.A.C.*, unreported High Court, Kinlen J. 9 March 2001 the High Court heard submissions from the Attorney General on whether residence should be recognized as a valid basis upon which a foreign divorce decree can be recognized. The High Court rejected residence as a basis for a foreign decree granted prior to 2 October 1986. In *D.T. v. F.L.*, Unreported High Court, 23 November 2001, Morris J. refused to recognize a foreign divorce granted after 2 October 1986 where the basis for recognition was residence as opposed to domicile. In both *R.B. v. A.S.*, [2002] 2 I.R. 428, and *P.K. v. T.K.*, [2002] 2 I.R. 186, Keane C.J. and Fennelly J. J. respectively stated obiter that the only basis for the valid recognition of a foreign divorce is the domicile of one of the parties in the jurisdiction granting the divorce. No other basis will suffice. As a result of the passing of the referendum on 24 May 2019, it is likely that the domicile rules for recognition of foreign divorces will be abolished and replaced with the concept of habitual residence.

172. [1993] 2 IR 476.
173. [2000] 1 ILRM 107.

237. The 1986 Act also recognizes divorces granted in a jurisdiction where neither spouse is domiciled in Ireland but the divorce is granted in another jurisdiction in which neither spouse is domiciled but the divorce is recognized as valid in the jurisdiction in which either spouse is domiciled. In these circumstances, the foreign divorce is capable of recognition in this jurisdiction.

238. A foreign divorce may be refused recognition where:

(a) the divorce is obtained by fraud in the jurisdiction granting the divorce;
(b) the divorce is obtained contrary to natural or constitutional justice;
(c) a spouse is forced by duress to institute divorce proceedings;
(d) estoppel of record will not prevent a decree of divorce being refused recognition where it can be shown that the foreign court had no jurisdictional competence to grant the decree;
(e) a spouse will not be prevented from challenging the validity of a foreign divorce at a later time despite having actively participated in obtaining the divorce. In this way the spouse is not estopped by his or conduct in seeking the divorce from challenging the recognition of the divorce and the court can thus refuse to recognize the divorce.

239. On 1 March 2005, Council Regulation 2201/2003 took effect in Irish Law. This regulation, otherwise known as Brussels II (A), requires the Irish courts to automatically recognize a divorce granted in any other Member State of the EU without the requirement of special or specific procedures.

VI. Judicial Separation

240. Under the Judicial Separation and Family Law Reform Act, 1989 and the Family Law Act, 1995, an Irish court may grant a decree of judicial separation where either of the spouses is domiciled or resident for a period of one year prior to the institution of the proceedings. Foreign decrees of judicial separation are capable of recognition where the decree is granted in a jurisdiction in which the spouses are domiciled. English law suggests that recognition should be afforded to foreign decrees based on the residence of both spouses in the jurisdiction granting the decree and on the residence of the respondent alone but not that of the residence of the petitioner.

VII. Financial Relief after Foreign Divorce or Legal Separation

241. The Family Law Act, 1995 provides for the making of financial relief orders against a party resident who is domiciled or who has property in this jurisdiction on foot of a foreign decree of divorce or separation. Prior to the introduction of this Act, the only means of obtaining financial relief was to seek to enforce an order of a foreign court or to rely upon the reciprocal arrangements between Ireland

and the United Kingdom and more recently the Maintenance Act, 1994, which gives effect to the Rome and New York Conventions on the recovery abroad of maintenance.

242. The Family Law Act, 1995 makes provision for the making of 'relief orders'. An application only can be made where:

(a) the foreign divorce or separation which is capable of recognition, was granted or the parties separated after the commencement of the Act;
(b) where a foreign divorce or separation is not capable of recognition, the parties may apply for an Irish divorce or legal separation;
(c) a party who remarries may not bring an application for a 'relief order' but the other party who does not remarry may bring an application.

243. The court has jurisdiction to make a 'relief order' where:

(a) either spouse was domiciled in the State at the date of the application for a 'relief order' or was domiciled in this jurisdiction on the date on which the divorce or legal separation took effect in the jurisdiction granting the divorce or legal separation;
(b) either of the spouses was ordinarily resident in the State for a period of one year prior to the dates mentioned above at (a);
(c) on the date of the institution of the proceedings as mentioned at (a) above, either spouse had a beneficial interest in land in the State.

244. Before an application for a relief order may be made, the applicant must first bring a preliminary application before the court showing that there is a 'substantial ground' for making a relief order. Where leave to bring a 'relief order' is granted, the court may make an interim maintenance order, either of a periodic or lump sum nature, provided that the court is satisfied that there is an immediate need of financial assistance for the applicant or dependent child.

245. Where the jurisdiction of the court is based upon (a) or (b) above, the court at the hearing of the relief order application may make any of the orders that a court may make on the grant of a judicial separation. The court also may order the making of provision for a spouse out of the estate of a deceased, separated, or divorced spouse. Where the jurisdiction of the court is based upon (c) above, the court is limited to making the following:

(a) lump sum order;
(b) a property adjustment order;
(c) extinguishing succession rights order;
(d) sale of an interest in a family home;
(e) an order making provision out of a spouse's estate.

246. Where the court makes a lump sum order or orders, the value of the order or orders cannot exceed in the case of the interest the spouse liable to make the payment or payments under the order or orders in the family home concerned is sold whether in pursuance of an order of the court or otherwise, the amount of the proceeds of the sale after the deduction therefrom of the costs thereof. In any other case, the amount cannot exceed such amount, in the opinion of the court, represents the value of the interest.

247. In deciding whether to make a relief order, the court must have regard to the factors a court considers on the making of ancillary relief orders after the grant of a judicial separation. If the application is in relation to a foreign divorce, the court must consider the duration of the marriage and the forfeiture of the opportunity or possibility of acquiring any benefit as a result of the grant of the divorce. Further, where a spouse is in desertion up to the institution of the foreign divorce or separation proceedings, the court may not make a relief order unless it would be unjust not to make an order.

248. The court must assess the needs of the applicant as against the means or income of the *liable* spouse. The court also must consider the extent to which the liable spouse has adhered to the orders of the foreign court and the extent to which the liable spouse will comply with the relief order made by the court. There are also the following factors that the court must consider:

(a) the connection the parties have with the State;
(b) the connection the parties have with the country other than the State in which the marriage was dissolved or in which the parties were separated;
(c) the connection the parties have with any other country other than the State;
(d) any financial benefit that the applicant or a dependent child has received or is likely to receive in consequence of the divorce or legal separation concerned or by virtue of any agreement or the operation of the law of country other than the State;
(e) where an order has been made by a foreign court requiring a party, or the parties, to make any payment or transfer any property for the benefit of the applicant or dependent child, the financial relief given by the order and the extent to which the order has been complied with or is likely to be complied with;
(f) any right that the applicant or dependent child has, or has had, to apply for financial relief from a party or the parties under the law of any other jurisdiction and, if the applicant or dependent child has omitted to exercise any such right, the reason for the omission;
(g) the availability in the State of any property in respect of which a relief order for the applicant or dependent child can be made;
(h) the extent to which the relief order is likely to be enforceable;
(i) the length of time that has elapsed since the date of the divorce or legal separation.

VIII. Recognition of Foreign Financial Orders

249. At common law an order of a foreign court for the payment of maintenance to a spouse or a child could only be enforced in this jurisdiction if the sum to be paid was final and conclusive. As an order for the payment of maintenance is capable of variation, it was thought that such was thus neither final nor conclusive. The uncertainty has been remedied by the Maintenance Act, 1994, which gives effect to the 1990 Rome Convention between Member States of EU on the Simplification of Procedures for the Recovery of Maintenance Payments and the 1956 New York Convention between Member States of UN on the Recovery Abroad of Maintenance. Arrears of maintenance that can be calculated as a lump sum are final and conclusive and enforceable in this jurisdiction.

250. Ireland has a reciprocal recognition and enforcement of maintenance orders arrangement with England, Wales, Scotland, and Northern Ireland. The reciprocal arrangement is given effect to in the Maintenance Orders Act, 1974.

251. The payment may be recognized and enforced where it is an order made incidental to a decision on the status of natural persons in either divorce or nullity proceedings. Where the spouses or parents have entered into a separation or maintenance agreement that has been made a rule of court, the agreement is recognized and enforceable. The Act only applies to the payment of maintenance and not to arrears of maintenance. An order may be refused recognition where:

(a) it would be contrary to public policy;
(b) where the order was made in default of appearance by the respondent who had insufficient time to arrange a defence;
(c) if the order is irreconcilable with a judgment given in a dispute between the same parties in this jurisdiction.

252. The Act provides a procedure whereby an application for maintenance may be commenced in this jurisdiction against a person liable to pay maintenance in another jurisdiction.

253. Jurisdiction of Courts and Enforcement of Judgments Acts, 1988 and 1993 (Brussels and Lugano Conventions).

254. These Acts give effect to the recognition and enforcement of maintenance orders between the Member States of the EU and European Free Trade Association (EFTA). The Acts only apply to maintenance payments, both periodic and lump sum, for the support of a spouse and/or children. Thus a lump sum payment ordered for a spouse as compensation for the loss of his or her marital status does not fall within the ambit of the Acts. Likewise property adjustment orders and orders declaring a spouse to be entitled to an interest in family property on the grant of judicial separation or divorce do not fall within the Acts.

255. An order may be refused recognition on the basis of the three grounds set out above in relation to the Maintenance Orders Act, 1974 in addition to the following grounds:

(a) if the court of the State of origin, in order to arrive at its judgment, has decided a preliminary question concerning the status or legal capacity of natural persons, rights in property arising out of a matrimonial relationship, wills or succession in a way that conflicts with a rule of private international law of the State in which the recognition is sought, unless the same result would have been reached by the application of the rules of private international of that State;
(b) if the judgment is irreconcilable with an earlier judgment given in a non-Contracting State involving the same cause of action and between the same parties, provided that this latter judgment fulfils conditions necessary for its recognition in the State addressed.

256. Where proceedings between the same parties are issued in more than one Member State, only the Member State first seized with the proceedings has jurisdiction and the proceedings in the other Member State must be stayed.

257. A maintenance application may be commenced in the Member State in which the applicant is resident or domiciled and is enforceable in the Member State in which the respondent is resident or domiciled.

258. The Maintenance Act, 1994 gives effect to the Rome and New York Conventions. Foreign maintenance orders, agreements, and court settlements are enforceable through the Central Authorities established in each Member State as are applications for the enforcement of maintenance orders, agreements, and court settlements in other Member States.

Chapter 3. Cohabitation Without Marriage

259. The non-marital family unit is not recognized in Irish law, though there are some protections afforded to cohabitants and children born of cohabiting parents. As seen above, Article 41 of the Constitution refers to the family as based upon marriage. Thus a non-marital family possesses no constitutional rights and does not have the same constitutional status as a marital family.[174] This was recently highlighted by the *Ennis v. Butterly*[175] case in which the court refused to enforce an agreement between a cohabiting couple on the basis that this was not enforceable at common law as offending against public policy. The court felt that this common law position was enforced by the protection afforded to the marital family under Article 41. The Civil Partnership and Certain Rights and Obligations of Cohabitants Act 2010 confers the same rights and protections afforded to married couples.

§1. Guardianship and Custody

260. This is set out in more detail in the following chapter but suffice it to say here that an unmarried father has no automatic right to guardianship and custody on the birth of a child unless he has cohabited with the mother of the child for a period of at least twelve months in which case he automatically acquires guardianship rights through the Child and Family Relations Act 2016. The mother possesses a unenumerated constitutional right to custody and care of her child.[176] An unmarried father has the right to apply to be appointed a guardian of his child[177] and until such occurs he possesses no rights save to be informed and consulted in any proposed adoption of the child by the mother.[178] Where an adoption is proposed, the unmarried father may apply to be appointed a guardian of his child, which, if granted, requires the father's consent for any valid adoption to take place.

§2. Financial Support

261. A cohabitant is entitled to financial support from the other cohabitant. A child born to an unmarried couple may have an application brought on its behalf for financial support under either the Family Law (Maintenance of Spouses and Children) Act, 1976 or the Guardianship of Infants Act, 1964. For the purposes of both pieces of legislation, a child is a person under the age of 18 or 23 if receiving full-time education.

174. *G. v. An Bord Uchtála* [1980] IR 32.
175. [1997] 1 ILRM 28.
176. *G. v. An Bord Uchtála* [1980] IR 32.
177. Section 6A of the Guardianship of Infants Act, 1964.
178. Adoption Act, 1998.

§3. Domestic Violence

262. The protection afforded by the Domestic Violence Act, 2018 is extended to non-marital couples. Homosexual relationships fall within the definition is now certain as a result of the same-sex marriage referendum. Where the application is for a barring or interim barring order, however, the applicant must establish:

(a) that he or she has been living with the respondent in an intimate relationship prior to the application for the barring order; and
(b) that the applicant possesses an interest in the property from which the respondent is sought to be excluded which is equal to or greater than that of the respondent's interest. This requirement does not apply for a safety order.

§4. Property Rights

263. The protections afforded to married couples under the family law legislation regarding property disputes are afforded to unmarried couples who cohabit or are in civil partnerships.[179]

§5. Succession Rights

264. Cohabitants have a right to succeed to the estate of a deceased cohabitant. 1. Children of unmarried parents, however, enjoy the same rights on succession as children born to married parents.[180]

---

179. *See Power v. Conroy*, Unreported High Court, February 1980 and *PD v. MC* [1994] 3 *The Family Law Journal* 91.
180. Part V of the Status of Children Act, 1987.

Chapter 4. Filiation

265. At common law the marital status at the time of conception or birth of a child determined the legal status of the child. A child born to unmarried parents was considered a child of no one (*filius nullius*) and was termed illegitimate. This common law position was to be reflected in the Constitution where the marital family is afforded the protection of Articles 41 and 42. The inferior legal position of the illegitimate child gave the child no rights in relation to his father's estate on death. The position of the illegitimate child was improved with the introduction of the Status of Children Act, 1987, which conferred upon all children regardless of their parents' marital relationship equal rights in relation to their parents. The concept and terminology of illegitimacy has been abolished by the Act. The Act also provides a mechanism for resolving disputes arising in relation to the parentage of a child. A child born to unmarried parents is, however, excluded from the constitutional protection afforded the family under Article 41.

266. Where a woman gives birth to a child, she is presumed at common law to be the mother of the child. Further, where the mother is unmarried, she is the sole legal guardian of the child and has a constitutional right to the custody and care of the child. The Child and Family Relationship Act 2015 provides for the parentage of children born by donor assisted human reproduction (DAHR) whereby the donor relinquishes parental rights by consent in acting as donor to the mother that gives birth to the child and her husband, civil partner or cohabitant.

267. At common law a child born to a married couple is presumed a child of the marriage and that the husband is the father of the child. The presumption arises where a child is born within ten months after the termination of a marriage. The presumption can be rebutted and burden of proof is on the balance of probabilities. Where a father's name is entered in the Registry of Births, he is presumed to be the father and this is likewise rebuttable.

268. Where a child's parentage is in dispute, under section 35 of the Status of Children Act, 1987, any child may apply to the Circuit Court for a declaration that a named person is his or her father or mother. Where a dispute arises between persons as to parentage, the court may direct the taking of blood samples to resolve the issue. There is no provision for the taking of DNA samples to resolve a dispute.

269. Married parents may register the birth of their child under the Births and Deaths Registration Acts, 1863–1996. If a child born to a married woman where the father is not the husband of the mother, such birth may be registered in the father's name provided the husband swears a statutory declaration that he is not the father and the mother swears a statutory declaration that she has been living apart from her husband for a period of more than ten months before the birth. A child born to unmarried parents may register the birth of the child at the joint request of the parents, at the mother's request with a statutory declaration as to the identity of the father and a declaration by the father acknowledging paternity. A birth may be registered at the father's request with a declaration as to paternity by him and confirmed by the mother or at the request of either the mother or father on production of a court order naming the father in proceedings concerning guardianship or maintenance.

270. Where a child is born outside marriage and the parents marry subsequent to the birth, the Legitimacy Act, 1931 presumes that the child is a child born of the marriage and the birth may be registered as a birth of a married couple.

271. At common law a child born to a void marriage was considered illegitimate. The Status of Children Act, 1987 provides that a father to a void marriage is presumed to be the joint guardian of the child of the marriage if he reasonably believed that the ceremony of marriage resulted in a valid marriage. Further there is a presumption that he so reasonably believes. A father to a voidable marriage retains his joint guardianship rights on the grant of a decree of nullity.

Chapter 5. Adoption

§1. Introduction

272. At common law a parent could not irrevocably transfer his or her parental rights and duties to a third party. Where a parent did attempt to transfer parental authority, the parent could reclaim the child at any time and the agreement was unenforceable as being considered contrary to public policy.

273. The First World War gave rise to numerous illegitimate births and made many children orphans. Adoption legislation was introduced in England and Wales in 1926, in Northern Ireland in 1929, and in Scotland in 1930. It was not until 1953 that the Adoption Act, 1952 came into effect providing for the lawful adoption of children by adopters. The delay in introducing legislation was due to the Catholic Church's objection to Protestant couples adopting Catholic children as well as to the interference with the rights of natural children to inherit from their natural parents.

274. All adoptions, whether domestic or foreign, are made by order of the Adoption Board. The validity of the Adoption Board was uncertain as it was considered to be exercising a judicial function and as it is not a court established under the Constitution, it would be acting unconstitutionally in making adoption orders. Article 37(1) retrospectively and prospectively validated all orders made by the Adoption Board. There are three forms of adoption: domestic voluntary adoptions, domestic involuntary adoptions, and recognition of foreign adoption.

275. When an adoption order is made, the adopters become the natural parents of the child with guardianship rights over the child. All legal rights and duties of the natural parent are terminated. The child is considered to be a natural child of the adopters and enjoys all the rights of a natural child of a family. The adopters and the adopted child are a family for the purposes of Article 41 of the Constitution. It is unlawful to advertise children for adoption and for a person making arrangements for an adoption to receive payment for the service.

§2. Requirements for Domestic Voluntary Adoption

276. The Adoption Acts from 1952 to 1988 have now been consolidated in the Adoption Act 2010. The Adoption Board is now titled the Adoption Authority of Ireland. The adoption laws have not been altered by the Adoption Act 2010.The adoption process is a two-stage process. The child first must be placed for adoption by the parent or guardian of the child. The placing for adoption requires the parent to consent to the placement. Once the child has been placed for adoption, the parent or guardian must then consent to the making of the order for adoption.

277. A child may be adopted if the child is under the age of 18 years who is an orphan, illegitimate, or who has been legitimated by the Legitimacy Act, 1931. A child cannot be lawfully adopted within six weeks of his or her birth. In the case of the adoption of a child over the age of 7, the Adoption Board must consider whether it should hear the views of the child.

278. The placing of a child for adoption requires the parent or guardian to be informed of the nature and consequences of an adoption. Further, the parent or guardian must be informed of their right to revoke their consent to the adoption and that if the parent or guardian refuses or fails to consent to the adoption order that an application may be made to the High Court to dispense with the necessary consent. A parent or guardian may not make the placement of the child dependent on the adopters fulfilling certain conditions. Only registered adoption societies or a health board may place a child for adoption.

279. Generally only a married couple over the age of 21 may adopt a child. There is no prescribed upper age limit for adopters. The adopters must be resident within the State and be of good moral character and capable of supporting the child. Widows, widowers, and separated spouses may adopt. At its discretion, the Adoption Board may authorize a person to adopt who does not meet these requirements.

280. Formerly an adoption order only could be made if the adopters were of the same religion as the child to be adopted. This was declared unconstitutional, as discriminating against adopters on ground of religion in *M. v. An Bord Uchtála.*[181] The law now required the consent of the parent or guardian to the adoption by adopters who are of a different religion from that of the child.

281. Where the parent or guardian refuses to consent to the adoption, the adopters may bring an application to dispense with the necessary consent under section 31 of the Adoption Act,2010. The court cannot dispense with the consent unless it is satisfied that the child has first been validly placed for adoption. A valid placing for adoption requires the parent or guardian consenting to such to be fully aware and informed of the nature and consequences of the placement, including knowledge that they can revoke their consent at any time prior to the adoption order being made. Further, the parent or guardian must be informed that an application to dispense with their consent may be brought if they fail or refuse to consent to the adoption, which will result in the parent or guardian losing all rights in relation to the child.

282. There has been a difference of judicial opinion as to the extent of the parent or guardian's level of understanding of these matters. In some cases it appears sufficient if the above information is given to the person placing the child for adoption, and mothers who were drug addicts and suffering from psychiatric illness have been held capable of consenting to the placement. In other cases, the court requires that the person placing for adoption fully understand the information and consequences.

181. [1975] IR 81.

283. Where the court is satisfied that a valid consent to place has been made, it may then dispense with the necessary consent to the adoption. In deciding whether to dispense with consent, the court determines this issue on the basis of what is in the best interests of the child's welfare.

§3. Involuntary Domestic Adoption

284. Such orders are rare and to date and there are very few reported cases where an order has been made. The Adoption Act, 2010 provides for the circumstances in which an involuntary adoption order may be made. This means that an adoption order may be made without the consent and with the objection of the parents or guardians. The requirements are very strict and the Adoption Board must first seek an order of the High Court authorizing the Adoption Board to make the adoption order. An involuntary adoption order may be made in relation to a marital or a non-marital child. In an application by the Adoption Board for an order authorizing the adoption, the High Court must be satisfied that:

(a) for a continuous period of not less than twelve months immediately preceding the making of the application, the sole parent or each of the parents for physical or moral reasons have failed in their duty towards the child;
(b) it is likely that such failure will continue without interruption until the child attains the age of 18 years;
(c) such failure constitutes an abandonment on the part of the parents of all parental rights, whether under the Constitution or otherwise, with respect to the child;
(d) by reason of such failure, the State, as guardian of the common good, should supply the place of parents;
(e) it considers other factors such as the present welfare of the child with the prospective adopters, the views of the natural parents and if appropriate the views of the child.

285. If an adoption order is found to be invalid for some reason, the court may decline to declare the order invalid if such is not in the best interests of the child. The court may make an order for custody without the need to institute separate proceedings.

§4. Foreign Adoptions

286. Owing to the very small number of domestic children being placed for adoption, prospective adopters seek to adopt children in foreign jurisdictions. Such adoptions, whilst valid in the jurisdiction in which the adoption is made, must be capable of recognition in this jurisdiction for the adoption to be valid in Irish law and thus confer legal status upon the adoptive parents and the child.

287. The Adoption Board maintains a register of all foreign adoptions. A foreign adoption will be recognized in this jurisdiction where the adopters were:

(a) domiciled in the jurisdiction where the adoption order was made;
(b) habitually resident in the jurisdiction where the adoption order was made;
(c) ordinarily resident in the jurisdiction where the adoption order was made for one year prior to the making of the order;
(d) adoptions effected prior to 1 July 1991, by persons domiciled, habitually or ordinarily resident in Ireland at the time of the making of the adoption order in the foreign jurisdiction must comply with the requirements for domestic adoptions.

288. The foreign adoption order must conform with the requirements for a valid domestic adoption order and include:

(a) the child must be under the age of 18;
(b) every consent required under the law of the jurisdiction in which the adoption was effected was obtained or dispensed with under the law;
(c) the adoption has the same legal effect in terms of determining and creating parental rights and duties in the foreign jurisdiction as a domestic adoption order;
(d) the law of the foreign jurisdiction, as far as was practicable, required the conducting of an inquiry into the adopters, the child, the parents or guardian and required the authority to consider the interests and welfare of the child;
(e) the adopters have not received or given any payment in respect of the adoption.

289. Where a foreign adoption is recognized in this jurisdiction, it has the same legal effect as a domestic adoption order.

§5. Consequences of Adoption

290. The consequences of an adoption order are that it makes the adopted child a natural child of the adopters. The natural parent or guardian's legal rights and duties towards the child are terminated. The adopted child may inherit from his adoptive parents as if a natural child of the family. Any order for maintenance against the natural father of the adopted child ceases to have effect, as does any order under the Child Care Act, 1991. Where the natural parents of the adopted child marry after the adoption, the adopted child is unaffected by the marriage. If the natural parents marry before the adoption of the child occurs, however, the father's consent to the adoption is necessary. The rights of the single father to apply for guardianship are extinguished on the making of an adoption order but he must be informed of the proposed adoption and be given an opportunity to be heard at the adoption and to apply for guardianship.

Chapter 6. Parental Authority, Guardianship, Custody, Access, and Matters Relating to Children

§1. Parental Authority and Guardianship

291. The law relating to children specifically revolves around the sole issue of their welfare. Any dispute concerning a child centre upon the issue of the welfare of the child and what is considered best for the welfare of a child. This approach to children is embodied in the Guardianship of Infants Act, 1964, which is the main piece of legislation concerning children.

292. In Irish law, guardianship is the term that signifies the rights and duties that parents possess in relation to their children. Only a person who has the right to guardianship may exercise the various rights that accompany guardianship. Guardianship is a broad concept that entitles parents to exercise the right to custody (physical control) of a child. It also embodies the right to determine how a child should be brought up in terms of physical, moral, social, and religious education.

293. At common law the father was the sole legal guardian of his legitimate child and this right could only be removed in rare circumstances. A mother possessed no rights unless the father died. The Courts of Equity, however, considered that they could exercise supreme control over the parent/child relationship and did so on the basis of the welfare principle. This principle requires the court to consider as first and of paramount importance the welfare of the child and is the fundamental basis upon which disputes concerning children are resolved today. The superior position of the father and the absolute nature of his rights over the child were gradually removed so that with the introduction of the Guardianship of Infants Act, 1886, there was almost equality of rights between parents.

294. The introduction of the Constitution in 1937 provided for the right to equality and the parental right to educate children. The case law subsequent to the introduction of the Constitution established that married parents have equal legal and constitutional rights in relation to their children.

295. Whilst the rights of parents vary according to their marital status, the rights of all children regardless of their parents' marital status are treated equally before the law. The law, however, is not obliged to treat all children identically.

296. Children, as citizens, possess important constitutional rights to education as set out in Article 42 and to what are described as natural and imprescriptible rights. Article 40 also confers unenumerated personal rights of a constitutional status. Some of the rights identified include the right to be born, to be fed, to live, to be reared, to be educated, to work, to medical treatment, and to realize their personality and dignity as a human being. Perhaps the most important constitutional right of a child is the right to be part of the marital family and access to his or her parents. Where there is a failure to provide any of these rights, Article 42(5) of the Constitution authorizes the State to intervene to vindicate the child's rights.

297. The rights that parents possess in relation to their children depend upon the marital status of the parents. All married parents, with or without children, constitute a family for the purposes of the protection of Article 41 of the Constitution. Such parents have in addition to rights conferred by statute, specified constitutional rights in relation to their children. Not only is the family protected by the Constitution, but the Constitution confers important rights upon the parents. The most important of these are the rights to guardianship and custody as well as the right to bring up and educate their children. These constitutional rights are reflected in the Guardianship of Infants Act, 1964, which confers equally upon married parents' joint guardianship of their children as against all other persons. Where spouses separate or divorce, they retain their rights to guardianship but may be declared unfit to have custody of a child. Parents to void and voidable marriages retain their rights to guardianship.

298. A constitutionally recognized family is not limited to married parents with natural children born to the marriage but includes a married couple who adopt children, widows, widowers, orphans of deceased married parents, separated parents, and perhaps divorced parents.

299. An unmarried mother has a constitutional right to the custody and care of her child but is not recognized as a family under the Constitution. An unmarried mother is the sole legal guardian of her child under the Guardianship of Infants Act, 1964 and thus has exclusive control and decision-making authority in relation to her child.

300. An unmarried father possesses no constitutional but does possess a legal right to guardianship or custody of his child under Section 43 of the Child and Family Relationship Act 2015. He also has the right to apply to be appointed as a guardian of his child where he has not cohabited with the mother of the child for a period of twelve months. The success of such an application to be appointed a guardian depends upon the nature and duration of the relationship with the mother of the child and in particular whether the decision to conceive the child was a joint and planned decision by the parents. An important factor in determining whether an unmarried father should be appointed a guardian of his child is where the mother proposes to place the child for adoption. Prior to the introduction of the Adoption Act, 1998, the unmarried father had no right to object to the adoption or to be heard in the adoption process. The unmarried father was not recognized as a legal relative of the child. The Adoption Act, 1998 was introduced as a result of the case *Keegan v. Ireland*[182] in which both the domestic laws concerning the rights of the father to form a family and the adoption process were found to breach Article 8 (right to family life) and Article 6 (right to fair procedures) of the European Convention for the Protection of Human Rights and Fundamental Freedoms. The Adoption Act, 1998 now provides that the unmarried father must be notified of the proposed adoption and informed of his right to apply for guardianship. He is also entitled to participate at the adoption hearing.

182. (1994) 18 EHRR 342.

301. Relatives of a child now have the right apply for access to a child. The Children's Act, 1997 requires a relative to first seek leave of the court to apply for access. Where leave to apply is granted, the application may be heard, but this does not necessarily mean that the relative will be granted access to the child. Any guardian of the child may object to either leave being granted or to the court ordering access.

302. Where a parent possesses the right to guardianship, that person, either jointly or alone, has the right to physical custody of the child and to determine how the child should be brought up and educated, including the moral, physical, social, and religious education of the child. The guardian also has the right to deal with child's property, to consent to medical procedures, and to the provision of a passport for the child. A guardian also has the right to agree to confer exclusive custody of the child to the other guardian or parent. A guardian also may also appoint a guardian to act after his or her death. A guardian has the right to consent to the adoption of the child.

303. The exercise of the right of custody by a parent or guardian is fundamental to invoking the protection of the Hague Convention on International Child Abduction, which provides a summary procedure for the return of children who are wrongfully removed from their jurisdiction of habitual residence. This Convention has been given effect in Irish law by the Child Abduction and Enforcement of Court Orders Act, 1991. As seen above, only a guardian has the right to exercise custody, and thus the unmarried father is very vulnerable in Irish law under the Convention where the mother of the child removes the child to another jurisdiction.

§2. Custody Disputes

304. Where a dispute arises in relation to the custody or welfare of a child, section 11 of the Guardianship of Infants Act, 1964 provides the mechanism for resolving the dispute before the court. This power of the court and the other powers that it possesses in relation to children are dealt with below.

305. There are a number of statues under which the powers of the courts may be invoked to determine the issue of the welfare or custody of a child. The power of the court is considerable and can vary depending on the circumstances of the case. Regardless of how the issue of the child's custody or welfare comes before the court, generally the sole consideration for the court is the welfare of the child. This is commonly known as the welfare principle and has both a statutory and a constitutional basis. 'Welfare' encompasses the moral, social, intellectual, and physical development of the child.

306. The primary means of resolving disputes between guardians who are the parents is under section 11 of the Guardianship of Infants Act, 1964. The court may make any order as it thinks proper regarding the custody or access of the child. The court may thus make an order granting custody to one parent or make an order that the parents have joint custody but that one parent should have primary control of the child. The court also may order the terms of access that a parent has in relation to the child. The right to access is a right of the child and not of the parent.

307. The issue of a child's welfare can arise and be determined by the court in any of the following family law proceedings:

(a) Section 11 of the Guardianship of Infants Act, 1964 in an application by a parent who is a guardian of the child.
(b) Section 6A of the Guardianship of Infants Act, 1964 in an application by the unmarried father of a child for guardianship.
(c) Section 11 B of the Guardianship of Infants Act, 1964 in an application by a relative for access to a child.
(d) Section 5 of the Family Law (Maintenance of Spouses and Children) Act, 1976 in an application for financial support of a dependent child.
(e) Section 5 of the Family Home Protection Act, 1976 in an application to protect against loss and interest in the family home. (f) Applications for judicial separation under the Family Law Reform Act, 1989 and the Family Law Act, 1995.
(f) Applications for Divorce under the Family Law Divorce Act, 1996.
(g) Applications for orders against domestic violence under the Domestic Violence Act, 1996.
(h) Adoption hearings under the Adoption Acts, 1952–1991.
(i) In applications under the Child Care Act, 1991 where the State intervenes to safeguard the welfare of children.
(j) In nullity petitions, there is no provision to deal with the issue of the children's welfare. A separate application under the Guardianship of Infants Act, 1964 must be made in the event of a dispute.

308. In deciding the issue of the welfare of a child, the courts have identified a number of factors that may affect the child's welfare. The factors are considered collectively and importance is not afforded to one factor over the others. The following are the factors that the courts have identified in cases concerning children's welfare:

(a) The tender years rule. This presumes that mothers are generally better capable of providing for the welfare of small children. This is not a legal absolute and fathers have been granted custody of small children.
(b) Ability to care for a child. The fact that one spouse is financially stronger than the other is irrelevant as this imbalance can be redressed by an order for maintenance. Where a spouse suffers from a mental or physical disability, this may affect their ability to provide for the child but does not automatically prevent a parent being granted custody.
(c) Sibling unity. This is an important factor as being in the company of his or her siblings enhances the social and emotional development of a child. Courts are thus reluctant to separate siblings in determining custody disputes.
(d) Continuity of care. It is considered harmful to the general development of a child to disrupt the bond and identity that a child develops with a parent who

has been granted custody. It is rare to order a change in custody from one parent to the other except where such is necessary to secure the welfare of the child.
(e) Parental conduct. The conduct of parents towards one another is irrelevant save where it affects the child's welfare. Where a parent behaves inappropriately towards a child, the parent's behaviour is a very relevant factor in determining custody. The courts are very aware to false allegations of sexual abuse made by one parent against the other, but all such allegations are carefully considered and generally require proof on the balance of probability that sexual abuse has occurred to consider this as a relevant factor.
(f) Religious education. A court will not interfere with the parent's decision as to the faith in which a child should be educated. Parental agreements as to religious education are enforceable.
(g) Moral welfare. Whilst the courts are divided as to the degree to which an extramarital relationship affects a child's moral welfare, the courts do all generally agree that such is harmful.

309. In disputes concerning children, the courts may appoint a guardian *ad litem* to advise the court on the child's welfare. The appointment is at the discretion of the court and arises in special circumstances whereby it is necessary in the best interests of the child. In deciding whether to appoint a guardian *ad litem*, the court is specifically obliged to consider:

(a) The age and understanding of the child.[183]
(b) Any welfare report furnished to the court.[184]
(c) The welfare of the child.[185]
(d) The extent to which a child should be given an opportunity to express his or her own wishes considering any views contained in a welfare report.[186]
(e) The submission of any party to the proceedings on the appointment of a guardian *ad litem*.[187]

310. Further, the courts may entertain the wishes of the child, but this depends upon the child's age and maturity. A court will always be reluctant to involve a child in court proceedings and will only do so in rare circumstances.

311. In all disputes concerning the custody of children, the parents' legal advisers are obliged to discuss an alternative dispute resolution with the parent.

183. *Ibid.*, s. 28(2)(a) as amended by s. 11 of the Children Act, 1997.
184. *Ibid.*, s. 28(2)(b) as amended by s. 11 of the Children Act, 1997.
185. *Ibid.*, s. 28(2)(c) as amended by s. 11 of the Children Act, 1997.
186. *Ibid.*, s. 28(2)(d) as amended by s. 11 of the Children Act, 1997.
187. *Ibid.*, s. 28(2)(e) as amended by s. 11 of the Children Act, 1997.

§3. CHILD ABDUCTION

312. Criminal and civil procedures and remedies exist to prevent the abduction of a child and his or her transfer out of the jurisdiction, and to secure the return of a child unlawfully retained within the jurisdiction. In the case of a child born within marriage, either parent may, in the absence of a court order to the contrary and with the consent of the other parent, remove the child from the jurisdiction. An unmarried mother does not require the consent of the natural father unless he has been made a guardian or granted custody rights. A child who is a ward of court may not be removed from the jurisdiction without permission of the court. A parent who believes that the other parent may be about to remove a child from the jurisdiction may apply under section 1 of the Guardianship of Infants Act, 1964 for an order prohibiting such removal except with the consent of either the applicant or the court. The court may order the respondent parent to relinquish any passport issued in respect of the child. A parent who breaks an order prohibiting removal of a child, or any person who knowingly assists him or her in so doing, is guilty of contempt of court.

313. The Adoption Act, 1952 makes it a criminal offence for any person to remove from the state a child below the age of seven who is an Irish citizen, except with the approval of a parent, guardian, or relative of the child. Sections 16 and 17 of the Non Fatal Offences Against the Person Act, 1997 makes child abduction an offence committed respectively by a parent or by any other person. A conviction on indictment can result in a maximum seven-year prison sentence. The common law offences of false imprisonment and kidnapping also may be relevant.

314. The Child Abduction and Enforcement of Custody Orders Act, 1991 brings into effect the Hague Convention on the Civil Aspect of International Child Abduction of 1980, and the European Convention on Recognition and Enforcement of Decisions concerning Custody of Children and on Restoration of Custody of Children of 1980. The High Court is given jurisdiction to hear applications under both Conventions. The central authority in both cases is the Minister for Justice, Equality and Law Reform. The great majority of cases are in practice dealt with under the Hague Convention. Article 13(b) of the Hague Convention, relieving the requested state of the duty to order the return of the child where 'there is a grave risk that his or her return would expose the child to physical or psychological harm or otherwise place the child in an intolerable situation', has been invoked successfully in a number of cases in which violent conduct on the part of the applicant featured. Article 20, allowing the requested state to refuse a return order where this would not be permitted by its 'fundamental principles', was unsuccessfully invoked in the Supreme Court in *CK v. CK.*[188] It had been argued that the children's rights under the Irish Constitution required the court to carry out a full inquiry into their welfare. In the context of Article 10(1)(a) of the European Convention, the Supreme Court has decided that it is not manifestly incompatible with Irish law to comply with a natural father's application to enforce an access order made in his favour. The Supreme

188. [1994] 2 IR 250.

Court has handed down a number of important decisions on the Hague Convention. In *HI v. MG*,[189] the court held that only de jure custody rights are recognized by the convention and enforceable through the courts. There an unmarried father failed to have return to New York his son whom he had lived with for some six years. The court did not recognize the de facto parental rights exercised by the father. In *T v. O*,[190] the High Court held that Article 6(2) of the Treaty of European Union gave effect to the case law of the European Convention of Human Rights, which has consistently held that unmarried fathers have the right to family life under the convention. In this regard, the father in this case did exercise rights of custody for the purposes of Article 2(11) of Council Regulation 2201/2003. Similarly, in *SH v. LH*,[191] a married father serving a prison sentence during which time he had limited visits from his children was exercising rights of custody owing to the fact that he was a married father. Perhaps the most significant decision is *LP v. NP*,[192] where the often-endorsed use of undertaking in child abduction cases was cautioned in this case. Here a child sexual abuse by the father was suspected by Italian authorities. The High Court ordered the return of the child to Italy subject to the father giving a number of undertakings. On return to Italy, the father the failed to abide by the undertakings given to the Irish court, which ultimately resulted in the child being taken from her mother and placed in State care. The main difficulty was that the Italian Civil Code did not recognize the concept of undertakings used in the common law system and there was no legal mechanism for recognition or enforcement of the undertakings given to a foreign court. This has been resolved by Council Regulation 2201/2003 giving legal recognition to the concept of an undertaking given in abduction cases by a parent.

315. Legal aid is available for applications under the Conventions.

§4. Wardship

316. The High Court and the Circuit Court also may rely upon the wardship jurisdiction to deal with any matter concerning the child's welfare. The wardship jurisdiction stems from the State's obligation as Sovereign, as *parens patriae* to protect the person and property of its subjects, who are incapable of caring for themselves or their property. The wardship jurisdiction is invoked particularly for those of unsound mind and children. Originally, the wardship jurisdiction was used by the courts to administer a child's property. Now a child does not require property for the court to make the child a ward of court. The effect of making a child a ward of court is to transfer the guardian's rights to the court. Where a child is made a ward of the court, the court retains exclusive jurisdiction over the child and may make any decision of any nature concerning the child. The court may order who has custody of the child and for how long. It can order how the child is to be educated,

189. [2000] 1 IR 110.
190. [2007] IEHC 55.
191. [2000] 2 ILRM 448.
192. Unreported High Court, 14 Oct. 1998.

where the child resides, and how the child's property is to be administered. Any requirement ordered by the court must be complied with. The jurisdiction exercised by the court in wardship is unlimited and broader than the discretion conferred by the court under the Guardianship of Infants Act, 1964. In exercising the wardship jurisdiction, the court is obliged to consider the child's welfare as the first and paramount consideration.

§5. Obligation of the State towards Children

317. Article 42(5) of the Constitution imposes a constitutional obligation to provide for children where their parents have failed to do so. This obligation authorizes the State to interfere with the rights of marital and non-marital parents to secure the health and welfare of children who require protection and care. In addition to the wardship jurisdiction, which may be invoked to safeguard children whose health or welfare is at risk, the Child Care Act, 1991 provides a number of remedies to provide for children whose health or welfare is at risk. By virtue of Article 42(5) of the Constitution, the State has provided for involuntary adoption of children with the Adoption Act, 1988.

318. The Child Care Act, 1991 replaced the Children Act, 1908 and is a very comprehensive piece of legislation which safeguards the health and welfare of children. It does have severe deficiencies in not providing health board with the authority to civilly detain children in high support units, which are in effect civil prisons that provide essential psychological, medical, and rehabilitation services to severely disturbed children who must be detained to prevent them from harming themselves.

319. The Child Care Act, 1991 confers upon health boards the duty to promote and secure the welfare of children. A child is any person under the age of 18. Where a person is over the age of 18 but suffers from a mental or physical disability, such a person is considered a child for the purposes of the Act. The exercise of the powers and duties conferred on the health board under the Act are subject to the health board having regard to both the welfare of the child as the first and paramount consideration and the legal rights of parents. Where it appears to a health board that the welfare of a child so requires it, it can seek to have the child voluntarily placed in care by the child's parents. Where the parents are unwilling to place a child voluntarily in care, the health board may invoke a number of powers to bring the child into care. A health board can seek from the District Court any of the following orders:

(a) An emergency care order where there is an immediate and serious risk to the health or welfare of a child. Such an application can be made without notice to the parents but they must be informed that the order has been made. The court on making the order may withhold the location of the child from the parents and prevent or allow access by the parents to the child. The court also may direct that the child undergoes psychiatric or medical treatment and assessment. An emergency care order is valid for eight days. The application is made under section 13 of the Act.

(b) An interim care order must be sought where an emergency care order is granted and can only be sought where a care order will be sought. The grounds upon which an order may be granted are where the child is or has been assaulted, ill-treated, neglected, or sexually abused. Further, where the health, development, or welfare is being avoidably impaired or neglected, a court may grant an interim care order. The order is valid for eight days and requires the parents to consent if an extension of the order is required. The health board must seek the court's direction for providing medical and psychiatric treatment for the child. The application is made under section 17 of the Act.

(c) A care order, if granted, may be indefinite in duration. The grounds for the order are the same as those for an interim order. Where a care order is made, the health board has authority over the child as if the health board were a parent of the child. It can thus provide the necessary consent for medical procedures and examination. Whilst the Act specifically confers autonomy upon the health board in relation to the child, the court retains considerable control over the child to the extent that a court can direct the health board to carry out certain tasks and functions in relation to the child. The application is made under section 18 of the Act.

(d) Where it appears to a court that a care order is inappropriate in the circumstances, it may grant a supervision order. This enables the child to remain with his or her family subject to supervision by social workers. The application is made under section 19 of the Act.

320. At the hearing of an application for any of these orders, the court may order that a guardian *ad litem* be appointed for the child. The guardian ad litem reports to the court on the child's welfare and both the child and the guardian ad litem may have legal representation. Further, where the court considers it appropriate, the court may consider the wishes of the child.

321. The Children Act, 1997 has made hearsay evidence admissible in such cases. Before the court admits hearsay evidence, the court must first assess whether the child is competent to give oral evidence before the court. The general principle is that it is not in the best interests of the child's welfare to have the child give evidence, and courts are reluctant to have children participate in proceedings. Where the court decides to admit hearsay evidence, it must then assess what weight and credibility to attach to the evidence. Hearsay evidence arises most often in cases of child sexual abuse where the child reveals to a third party that they have been abused. The health board will then seek to have the third party give evidence as to what was told to them by the child. The Supreme Court has indicated in *Re M., S. & W. (infants)*[193] that the third party giving the evidence should be an expert akin to that of a child psychologist or psychiatrist and particularly so in cases involving

193. [1999] 2 ILRM 321.

allegations of sexual abuse. The third party may be cross-examined in his testimony and any reports or videotapes of interviews must be made available to the person against whom the allegations are made.

322. The Gardai (police) are also empowered under section 12 of the Child Care Act, 1991 to enter with force if necessary, with or without a warrant, and remove a child to whose health or welfare there is an immediate and serious risk. Further, there must be insufficient time to seek an emergency care order to invoke this power. The Gardai must then deliver the child to a health board that must then seek an emergency or interim care order.

323. When a child is brought into care, the health board may determine, subject to any direction of the court, with what care to provide the child. Health boards may place the child in foster care, residential care, or with relatives.

324. Prior to the enactment of the Children Act, 2001 where a child was severely disturbed to the extent that their life was in danger and required secure detention, the health board had to apply to the High Court to seek an order authorizing the health board to place the child in secure detention, which was usually a children's prison or the Central Mental Hospital. The application had to be made to the High Court, as there was no authority conferred on the health board under the Child Care Act, 1991 to civilly detain children, nor did the court possess the authority to make orders detaining children in suitable facilities.

325. The central problem in these cases, of which there are many, is the abject failure of the State to provide secure detention units. The Supreme Court in *DG (a minor) v. The Eastern Health Board, Ireland and the Attorney General*[194] upheld the validity of the detention in a juvenile prison but ordered that such could be for a very temporary period. The reason for authorizing the detention was the court's constitutional obligation to vindicate the rights of the child even if this required infringing on the child's constitutional rights to liberty and a good name. Subsequently in *TD v. Minister for Education*,[195] the Supreme Court allowed an appeal from the High Court where the judge has granted an injunction against the Minister for Education, directing him to make available the necessary resources to provide appropriate accommodation for severely disturbed children. The Supreme Court was of the view that the injunction breached the doctrine of the separation of powers and the judge has exceeded his authority by so doing. The DG case was brought before the ECHR[196] where Ireland was found to have breached the applicant's right to liberty by having him detained in a juvenile prison. Since these decisions, the Children Act, 2001 has brought into effect as part IVA of the Child Care Act, 1991, which authorized the secure detention of children under Special Care Orders. Children are to be detained in Special Care Units. The problem, however, persists not so much from a legal perspective but from a practical one. Staffing of these units is

194. [1998] 1 ILRM 241.
195. [2000] 4 IR 259.
196. *DG v. Ireland* (2002) 35 E.H.R.R. 33.

very difficult in terms of recruitment and retention of staff. So whilst there are special units provided, they are often not operating owing to the lack of staff. Amendments to the Child Care Act 1991 in 2007, 2011 and 2013 now provide the courts with the authority to order the secure detention of children in high support units the use of special care orders.

Part III. Matrimonial Property Law

Chapter 1. Matrimonial Property Dispute Resolution

§1. Property Disputes

326. At common law, a married woman did not possess the legal capacity to own or acquire property. Her legal capacity was entirely dependent upon her husband. There was no principle of the right to own separate property. When a woman married, all her property vested in her husband who had sole authority in relation to his wife's property during his lifetime. If the husband died then the property reverted to his wife. In order to dispose of property, a wife was obliged to join her husband in the transaction.

327. These somewhat harsh common law rules were lessened by the role of Equity, which created the notion of property for 'separate use' by a wife. This notion operated by transferring her property to trustees or to her husband where it could apply for her 'separate use'. In this way, the property remained her separate property and she could deal with as if she were unmarried. In effect, a wife had a limited legal capacity to enter contracts but the contract only bound her property and not the wife personally as the husband remained personally liable for his wife.

328. The Married Women's Property Acts conferred upon a wife both the legal capacity to own separate property and to enter and be personally liable in contract. There remained for the benefit of a wife the principle of *restraint upon anticipation*. This protected a wife where she was influenced by her husband or where she unwisely disposed of property. The effect of the principle was to declare the transaction void. The Conveyancing Act, 1881 authorized the courts to remove a restraint and to give effect to the transaction if the wife consented and the transaction was for her benefit.

329. Prior to the introduction of the current form of judicial separation and divorce applications, disputes in relation to marital property were resolved by the Married Women's Status Act, 1957. This Act has been repealed by the Family Law Act, 1995, which provides for a new method of determining such disputes that do not arise in the course of judicial separation or divorce proceedings. Section 36 allows either spouse to bring an application to either the Circuit Court or the High Court to determine any question arising between them as to the title to or possession of any property.

330. The 1957 Act treated husband and wife as separate persons for the acquisition and disposal of property. A wife, by virtue of this Act, has full and independent legal capacity to enter and be bound in contract. The principle of restraint upon anticipation was also abolished. The 1957 Act did not confer upon a wife any ownership in property unless she separately acquired it. A wife did, however, benefit from the common law principles that she possessed a right to reside in the family home even if she had no legal or equitable interest in the property. Where she did possess a legal or equitable interest in the property, she possesses a right to reside there on the basis of that interest. Further, at common law the primary duty to provide a home lies with the husband but this right is only enforceable as against the husband.

331. The law as developed under the 1957 Act is largely redundant since the introduction of judicial separation and divorce, as the court possesses extensive powers to make orders in relation to property. The principles as developed by the courts, however, do provide a good background against which the current law operates.

I. Property Owned Solely by One Spouse

332. Where the legal title to property is held in the sole name of one of the spouses, common law presumed that that spouse owned the entire interest in the property. The view of the Irish courts, however, in this respect may be summarized as enquiring as to how the property was acquired by the spouses respective direct or indirect financial contributions rather than accepting that the title deeds to the property determine the ownership. A direct or indirect contribution by a spouse to the acquisition of a property entitles that spouse to claim a beneficial interest in the property. A direct contribution amounts to contributing to the deposit, the purchase price or the loan repayments of the property. In Ireland, the courts have expressly stated that it is futile to look for an agreement between the spouses as to how their contributions are to be reflected in the legal or beneficial ownership of the property. The leading decision in this regard is *Conway v. Conway*[197] the effect of which is to create a trust held by the husband in favour of the wife. The extent of the spouse's interest in the property is determined proportionally to the contribution made. There is an exception to these general principles, which is the *presumption of advancement.* This presumption operates only in favour of a wife and not in favour of a husband. Where a husband solely provides the purchase price for a property and transfers the entire legal interest in that property to his wife, he is presumed to advance to her the entire legal interest in the property. This presumption is rebuttable by the husband establishing that it was not his intention to confer the entire legal interest in the property upon his wife. As the presumption does not operate in favour of a husband, the presumption is considered to be unconstitutional in breaching the requirement of equality before law.

197. [1976] IR 254.

333. Indirect contributions by a spouse also entitle a spouse to claim an interest in the property. Where the contribution is indirect in nature, it must be in money or money's worth. Thus where one spouse pays all the mortgage or loan repayments and the other spouse discharges other household expenses such as food, utilities, school fees, and the like, such contributions have been held to entitle that contributing spouse to an interest in the property. Working without pay in a family business is also considered an indirect contribution *even though* there is no tangible positive financial contribution by the spouse to the property. The reason for conferring an interest in the property on the spouse in these circumstances is that the contributions made by that spouse relieve the other spouse of that financial burden and enable that spouse to contribute directly to acquiring the property.

334. Specifically excluded as an indirect contribution are improvements to property unless there is an express agreement as to how that improvement is to be reflected in terms of the legal ownership of the property. More controversial is the issue of work within the home as a wife and mother. In *B.L. v. M.L.*[198] the Supreme Court held that such a contribution could not be equated with a direct or indirect financial contribution. As a result of this decision, the Matrimonial Homes Bill, 1993 was introduced but referred by the President to the Supreme Court to assess its constitutional validity. The Supreme Court held that the effect of the Bill was to confer an automatic joint legal ownership of the family home, which was unconstitutional in usurping the autonomous decision-making authority of the family as guaranteed under Article 41 of the Constitution. These difficult issues, and the general principles, have been rendered redundant owing to the now expansive powers that the courts possess in relation to property adjustment orders and the factors that a court is obliged to consider in exercising such powers.

II. Jointly Owned Property

335. Where the legal title to a property is stated to be held jointly and both contribute to the acquisition or repayment of the loan on the property, then such is considered to amount to an intention that each spouse is to hold an equal beneficial interest in the property. If the purchase money is provided solely by the wife, the law presumes a resulting trust in her favour whereby the husband holds the beneficial interest on trust for her. However, where the husband solely provides the purchase price, the law presumes according to the *presumption of advancement* that the husband intended to vest a beneficial interest in his wife. The husband providing evidence of an intention not to benefit his wife may rebut this presumption. Whether a beneficial interest will be found in favour of both spouses in these circumstances ultimately depends upon the intention of the parties at time of the acquisition of the property.

198. [1992] 2 IR 77.

§2. Household Allowance

336. Historically at common law where a husband provided a wife with money to discharge household expenses and the wife acquired property with such money, the law presumed that the property acquired belonged to the husband, unless it was the husband's intention to make a gift to the wife. Section 21 of the Family Law (Maintenance of Spouses and Children) Act, 1976 provides that any property so acquired in this fashion shall be owned jointly by the spouses unless there is an agreement to the contrary.

§3. Protection of the Family Home

337. Where the legal title to the family home is held in the name of one spouse alone, then the Family Home Protection Act, 1976 requires the other spouse to consent in writing, prior to the conveyance of the property. Where there is no written consent to the conveyance, the transaction is void. The effect of this Act is to ensure that the family home cannot be sold without the wife's consent and knowledge. The Act does not confer any propriety rights upon a spouse. It merely confers a statutory right to veto the conveyance. The Act was introduced after a survey by the Commission on the Status of Women in 1972 revealed that the vast majority of family homes were held in the sole name of husbands.

338. Over the last twenty-nine years, considerable case law has developed on the interpretation of this Act. Central to the operation of the Act is the definition of the 'family home'. This is a very broad definition that encompasses any dwelling in which a married couple resides. To fall within the definition of a 'family home', the spouses must actually reside there at the time of the intended conveyance. Thus where a couple intend to reside in a property in the very near future but do not do so prior to the conveyance of that property such is not a family home for the purposes of the Act.

339. Only a conveyance by a spouse without the other spouse's prior written consent is void. The definition of 'conveyance' is extremely broad and covers any method of disposing of an interest in a family home. A spouse who conveys a family home must have an interest in the property before the Act operates. Thus, where the conveyance is effected by a third party who is the sole legal owner, the protection of the Act does not arise. Therefore, for example, where a limited company owns a property in which a married couple reside and the limited company conveys the property, then the prior written consent of a spouse is not necessary. A similar position arises where a husband or wife goes bankrupt and the Official Assignee is appointed. Where the Official Assignee conveys the property, such is not a conveyance by a spouse. A more problematic situation arises where a judgment mortgage is registered against a spouse's interest in the family home. Such arises where a spouse defaults on an unsecured loan and the creditor obtains judgment in the amount outstanding. That judgment may be registered against an interest in the family under the Judgment Mortgage (Irl) Acts, 1850 and 1858 the effect of which is to convey to the judgment mortgagee the defaulting spouse's interest in the family home. Such is not a conveyance by a spouse but a conveyance by operation of law. It should be noted, however, that the judgment mortgagee takes subject to any beneficial interest the other spouse may have in the property.

340. The nature of the consent to the conveyance has been extensively defined in *Bank of Ireland v. Smyth.*[199] Here the wife consented to a charge in favour of the bank but believed the charge related only to the lands surrounding the family home and not the family home. In these circumstances, the Supreme Court held that she had not provided a fully free and informed consent to the conveyance, which was declared void. The court stated that the bank, if it wished to acquire a binding charge over the property, should have ensured that the wife was fully aware of to what she was consenting.

341. There are exceptions to the requirement of a prior written consent provided for in section 3 of the Act:

(a) where there is an agreement to convey a property prior to the marriage but the transaction is not complete until after the marriage and the married couple have resided in the property during that time then such a conveyance is not caught by the Act and no consent is necessary;
(b) where the conveyance is to a *bona fide* purchaser for full value then the absence of a consent to the conveyance will not invalidate the conveyance. A *bona fide* purchaser is a person who has no knowledge that the property is a family home and purchases the property in good faith in these circumstances. It is very difficult, however, for a purchaser to establish that he has no knowledge that the property is a family home. The Conveyancing Act, 1882 imposes the doctrine of notice on purchasers who are obliged to make such enquiries that are reasonable. Further, notice may be imputed to the purchaser if such a fact has come to the knowledge of his legal advisor or would have if such enquiries had been made as ought reasonably have been made by his legal advisor. This confers substantial protection upon the spouse who has no legal interest in the family home and that spouse's position is further strengthened by section 12 of the Act, which allows a spouse to register a notice in the Registry of Deeds that a property is a family home within the meaning of the Act. In this way the title to the property will have attached to it the fact that it is a family home and where the obligatory search of title deeds is conducted by a solicitor in conveying a property, that solicitor will have notice of the property being a family home;
(c) a conveyance by someone other than a spouse such as a limited company, the Official Assignee in bankruptcy or a judgment mortgagee;
(d) a conveyance subsequent to a decree of judicial separation or divorce where the court has ordered the transfer to one spouse of the family. No consent by the other spouse is necessary in these circumstances.

199. [1995] 2 IR 459.

342. Where a spouse seeks to challenge the validity of a conveyance, such an action must be brought within six years of the conveyance. The Family Law Act, 1995 introduced this limitation period as the 1976 Act did not provide a time frame within which such a challenge should be brought.

343. Where a spouse omits or refuses to consent to the conveyance of a family home, an application may be brought to dispense with the spouse's consent. The consent may only be dispensed with where the spouse unreasonably withholds the necessary consent. Where the spouse is unreasonably withholding consent, the court is obliged to consider the respective needs and resources of the spouses and any dependent children and, where alternative accommodation is offered, the suitability of that accommodation.

344. An order dispensing with consent may also be sought where a spouse is either in desertion for a continuous period of one year or is incapacitated to the extent that the spouse cannot consent. An application for dispensing with consent must be brought prior to the effecting of the conveyance.

345. The Act further secures the position of a spouse to reside in the family home where the other spouse has placed at risk an interest in the family home. Section 5 authorizes the court to transfer the entire interest in the property to the spouse. A spouse seeking such an order must establish that the other's spouse's conduct amounts to an intention to deprive the spouse of the right to reside in the family home. If a spouse has lost the right to reside in the family home, the court may order the payment of compensation to the spouse who has been deprived of the right of residence. Section 6 further protects the position of a spouse by enabling that spouse to pay any liabilities due on the family home and the creditor is obliged to accept such payments as if they were made by the defaulting spouse.

Part IV. Succession Law

Chapter 1. Succession

346. The law in Ireland regarding Succession is contained in the Succession Act, 1965. This Act provides for the manner in which a person may dispose of their property, both real and personal, after their death. It further provides for who may inherit from a person on their death and for the share to which a spouse and children are entitled. The shares that a spouse and children are entitled to depend upon whether a deceased has made a valid and effective will.

347. There are two forms of succession dealt with by the Act, testate and intestate succession. Where a person dies, the property that they own is called their 'estate', which can then be distributed according to the wishes of the deceased as contained in the will or according to the rules of distribution provided for on intestate death. Where a person dies having made a valid and enforceable will, such a person is called a 'testator' or a 'testatrix' if female. Where a person dies having made no will or the will is invalid owing to some defect in its execution, the deceased is said to have died 'intestate'. A deceased may also die partly testate and partly intestate. This arises, for example, where a deceased makes a will only in relation to a portion of his estate. The remainder of the estate is distributed according to the rules on intestate succession.

348. The Act provides for a limited form of restricting the absolute right of a person to dispose of his property after his or her death. The common law in relation to succession recognized the absolute right of a testator to dispose of freely his or her property. The Roman law system, upon which the civil law systems of the countries of mainland Europe are based, imposed limitations upon the freedom to dispose of property by providing an entitlement for a surviving spouse and children to a fixed share of the testator's estate. This entitlement was known as the *legitima portio* and restricted the right of the testator to disinherit his spouse and children.

349. The Roman law and common law influences are reflected in the Act in that a surviving spouse is entitled to a minimum share of at least one-third of the testator's estate. Surviving children are not entitled to a minimum fixed share of their deceased parent's estate, but they do have the right to apply to court under section 117 of the Act for provision to be made to them where the court is satisfied that the deceased parent has failed to make proper provisions for the surviving child or children.

350. The justification for restricting freedom of disposing of property on death is Article 41 of the Constitution, which states that the family is a moral institution possessing inalienable and imprescriptible rights antecedent and superior to all positive law. To allow a spouse to disinherit his or her family would be at variance with this statement of principle. Further, the benefit that mothers provide to the family, which Article 41 considered to be their duty, would not be acknowledged if there was full freedom of disposing of property on death. In any event, the concept of restricting the right of a spouse to dispose of property on death was recognized by Irish law in the 'Custom of Ireland', which was abolished by the Irish Statute of Distribution, 1695 following the colonizing or 'Plantation' of Ireland by King Henry VIII.

Chapter 2. Intestate Succession

351. Where a person dies and has made no will or has made a will but the will fails to take legal effect, the person is said to die intestate. A person does not die intestate where the will is validly executed but is ineffective to dispose of the testator's property. A person may die wholly intestate or partly intestate. A person dies partly intestate where a valid will provides for the distribution for only part of the deceased's property. The Succession Act, 1965 simplified how an intestate's property should devolve on death by providing that all personal and real property of the intestate should vest in his personal representatives. Further, the Act provides how the property of the intestate should be disposed of. Prior to the introduction of the Succession Act, 1965, the rules governing the distribution of an intestate's personal property were contained in the Intestate Estates Act, 1954. Real property descended in accordance with the judge-made law of inheritance, which was formulated in the Inheritance Act, 1833. The main principles of the law of inheritance were:

(a) that the intestate's property descended to his blood relatives lineally and in this regard children and grandchildren were preferred to parents and grandparents;
(b) males were preferred to females where the principle of primogeniture operated to confer the intestate's entire property upon the first male born and in the event that the first male born predeceased the intestate, then the issue of the deceased's first born succeeded as against the other issue of the testator;
(c) widows were entitled to 'dower', which was a life estate in one-third of the intestate's property;
(d) widowers were entitled to 'curtesy', which was a life estate in the whole of the intestate's property.

352. The Succession Act, 1965 abolished the rules contained in the Intestate Estates Act, 1954 and the Inheritance Act, 1833. Once all expenses, debts and liabilities, and any legal right payable from the intestate's estate have been discharged, the estate of the intestate is distributed in the following order and in the shares specified:

(a) Spouse and issue:
  - where a spouse survives and there is no issue, the spouse is entitled to the entire estate;
  - where a spouse survives with issue, the spouse takes two-thirds of the estate with the remainder being divided equally amongst the issue;
  - where no spouse survives but issue do and are all in equal degree of relationship to the deceased, then the issue are entitled to the entire estate divided equally amongst them;
  - where no spouse survives and issue do, but the issue are not in equal degrees of relationship to the deceased, then the distribution is of the estate is *per stripes*. The effect of this is that the issue of the child of a deceased (i.e., the grandchild or children of the deceased) will take the share their deceased

parent is entitled to in equal shares. The former position under the Inheritance Act, 1833 provided that a wife that survived her husband was entitled to a priority charge of GBP 4,000 plus one-half of her deceased husband's estate, the remainder of the estate being divided amongst the deceased's next of kin in equal shares. In the case of a husband surviving his wife, he was entitled to the deceased wife's entire estate;

- prior to 1987, an illegitimate child was precluded from benefiting from the estate of their deceased intestate parent. The Status if Children Act, 1987 now provides that all children, regardless of whether their parents are married, may inherit from their deceased intestate parent. It should be noted, however, that section 117 does not apply to enable a deserving child to bring an application for a greater share than the fixed statutory share where the parent dies intestate. Further, the share a child is entitled to on intestacy may be reduced where the child has received permanent provision from the deceased during his or her lifetime. Both the child and any surviving issue of the child may receive the share on intestacy but reduced by the value of the permanent provision made to the child;

(b) parents surviving a deceased child who has no spouse or issue take equally if both parents are alive and solely if only one is alive. Previously where both parents survived, the father of the deceased inherited the whole estate. Where only the mother survived the child and the deceased had brothers and sisters, the mother shared equally with her other surviving children;

(c) where the deceased is not survived by any of the above, the brothers and sisters of the intestate shall inherit in equal shares. Where a brother or sister of the deceased predeceases the intestate, the children of the deceased brother or sister inherit in equal shares the share their parent would have been entitled to if alive at the death of the intestate. Where no brothers or sisters survive the intestate, the estate is divided between all nieces and nephews of the intestate;

(d) where none of the above survive the intestate, then the next of kin are entitled in equal shares. Next of kin are determined by who is closest, by degree, in blood relationship to the intestate. The nearest direct lineal relative inherits except where the relatives are in equal degree of relationship. For example, where a grandfather and an uncle survive an intestate, the grandfather is the nearest lineal relative by two degrees of blood relationship and the uncle by three degrees. Where a great-grandfather and an uncle survive the intestate, both are in equal degrees of blood relationship from the intestate but here the uncle is preferred to the great-grandfather;

(e) where the intestate has no next of kin, the State inherits the estate of the deceased. The Minister for Finance, however, has a discretion to waive the right of the State to inherit in favour of such person and upon such terms as he thinks proper.

Chapter 3. Testamentary Succession

§1. Wills

353. A 'will' is the term used to identify a legal document that contains the wishes of a person in relation to their property and how such is to be distributed after their death. Usually there is only one document that is the last will of the deceased, but there may be more than one document expressing the wishes of the deceased. Where there are other documents concerning the distribution of the deceased's property, these are commonly called 'codicils' and form part of the deceased's will.

354. There are two main characteristics of a will. The first is that a will only takes effect on the death of the testator. This means that the testator may dispose of property provided for in the will during his lifetime by *inter vivos* deed to a person other than the beneficiary under the will. This results in the beneficiary losing the device or bequest in the will. A will is thus declaratory of the testator's intention until his or her death.

355. The second characteristic of a will is that it is revocable prior to death and even if a will is stated to be irrevocable, such may still be revoked by the testator. The revocability of a will is subject to an action being brought against the personal representatives of the deceased where the testator has contracted to make a will and to devise or bequest a gift in favour of an individual. Even a promise to provide for an individual in a will, which is not enforceable as a breach of contract, may nevertheless be brought against the estate of the deceased. This often occurs in family settings where a child is promised a gift in parent's will where the child cares for a sick and elderly parent. The child's claim to a share in the estate of the deceased parent may be enforced by way of the doctrines of part performance, estoppel, or constructive trust. A further limitation on the right to revoke a will is the entering into of mutual will with another person. Such usually occurs between spouses whereby they agree to devise or bequest property to the surviving spouse, with the remainder of the estate to named beneficiaries who are usually the children of the marriage. A mutual will implies that neither party will revoke the will during their lifetime. Where a surviving party does revoke a mutual will, the beneficiaries may enforce their claim against the estate of the surviving party, which the court will uphold by imposing a trust in favour of the beneficiaries.

§2. The Making of a Will

356. Section 78 of the Succession Act, 1965 requires that for a will to be valid it must be in writing and:

(a) be signed at the foot or end thereof by the testator or by some person in his presence and by his direction;

(b) that the signature be made or acknowledged by the testator in the presence of each of two or more witnesses present at the same time, and each witness shall attest by his signature the signature of the testator, in the presence of the testator, but no form of attestation shall be necessary nor shall it be necessary for the witnesses to sign in the presence of each other.

357. The requirement of the will being in writing has been liberally interpreted and any form of writing is sufficient. The material upon which the will is written must be permanent, and even an empty eggshell upon which the terms of the will were written has been held to be a valid will. The language of the will must be at least intelligible and may be in any language. No particular form of words is necessary and the witnessing by a solicitor and his secretary of the deceased's instructions given at a consultation was held to constitute a valid will. The document need only be testamentary in character, and thus the absence of formal or technical language such as 'will', 'testament', and 'executor' is not necessary once the contents of the document indicate that it is of a testamentary nature in that the deceased sets out his intention as to how his property is to be disposed after his death.

358. The signature of the testator may take any form from a mark or a stamp to a pseudo name or initials. The signature may be partial or complete and may be assisted by another in his attempt to sign, but the testator must make some positive attempt to sign in these circumstances. The will can even be signed by another person on the direction of the testator. Whatever the form of the mark made to the will, it is essential that the mark made by the testator is intended to be his signature. The signature of the testator must be at the end of the will, but this requirement is broadly interpreted.

359. The signature must be witnessed by at least two persons. The witnesses must be present but need not see the act of signing. The witnesses must sign the will attesting that they have witnessed the signature of the testator. It is common to have a formal attestation clause. The only factors that make a witness incompetent are where the witness or his or her spouse is a beneficiary under the will and where the witness is blind.

360. Where there is a defect with the formal requirements of executing a will, the will is invalid. However, the courts adopt the presumption of due execution where at all possible and favour testacy against intestacy. The presumption is rebuttable and arises where a will has been executed in accordance with formalities.

361. Where a will is executed, its contents usually provide for how the testator's property is to be disposed of and is thus the only document containing the wishes of the testator in relation to his property. However, other documents may form part of the testator's will and have legal effect by the doctrine of incorporation by reference. There are two conditions that attach to the doctrine of incorporation by reference:

(a) the document to be incorporated must be in existence at the date of the will; and
(b) the document to be incorporated must be clearly identified in the will.

362. The courts have strictly interpreted these requirements.

363. In addition to these formal requirements, the testator must have an *animus testandi*. This is an intention to make a disposition of his property that will take effect after his death. It not necessary to establish that the testator intended to execute a valid will.

364. Section 71 of the Succession Act, 1965 provides that a will shall be made by a person who has reached the age of 18 or who is or has been married and is of sound disposing mind. Whether a person is of sound disposing mind largely depends upon whether the testator makes the will being aware that the document is to give effect to the deposition of his property after his death, and this is executed with understanding and reason. The relevant time at which the testator must be of sound disposing mind is the date of execution of the will. Thus a testator who suffers from a mental illness that impairs his or her ability to execute a will may nevertheless do so if at the time of execution of the will, the testator was lucid. Where the testator is elderly or infirm, the capacity to understand the contents of the will may be impaired and thus the *animus testandi* may be questioned. The instructing solicitor reading over the contents of the will to the testator may overcome this difficulty. A court may refuse to admit a will to probate in circumstances where the testator is elderly, infirm, and where the principal beneficiary under the will is the person who has drafted the will. Two general presumptions arise in these circumstances that oblige the person seeking to have the will admitted to probate must satisfy the court that the document is the last will of a free and capable testator. Further, where a party prepares a will under which he or she will benefit, such should arouse the suspicion of the court, which obliges the court to be vigilant in examining the evidence supporting the validity of the will, and the court should not admit the will until the suspicion is removed. The validity of a will also may be impugned where a person makes a claim of undue influence. Here, however, no presumption arises against the person whom it is claimed has unduly influenced the testator. The burden of establishing undue influence in the execution of a will rests with the person alleging it.

§3. Alterations and Revocation

365. Section 86 of the Succession Act, 1965 provides that alterations to a will made after the execution shall be invalid unless the alteration is signed by the testator and witnessed by the signature of each witness opposite or near such alteration. The alterations also may be attested to and witnessed in a memorandum, which refers to such alterations at the end of some other part of the will. Once the testator intends the alteration to form part of the will, the alteration can be admitted to probate. Usually the testator and the witnesses will mark their initials near or opposite such alterations. Any alteration must be significant to be considered by the court to form part of the will.

366. Where alterations are not attested to, there is a presumption that such alterations were made after the execution of the will and are thus invalid and do not form part of the will. Only slight evidence is necessary to rebut the presumption, and the courts have adopted a liberal approach in admitting evidence to rebut the presumption. Examples of evidence in rebuttal of the presumption are:

(a) the attesting witnesses stating that they observed the alterations prior to the execution of the will;
(b) the person who drafted the will states that the alterations were made prior to the execution of the will;
(c) the testator declares prior to execution of the will that alterations have been made.

367. The burden of establishing that the alteration was made prior to execution of the will lies with the person asserting the validity of the alteration. Circumstantial or extrinsic evidence may be relied upon to establish when the alteration was made. Where alterations are of no effect, the will can be admitted to probate and the alterations will be treated as blank spaces in the body of the will.

368. Alteration to a will may be validated by re-executing the will or by executing a codicil to the will, which validates the alterations.

369. A will is revocable at any time during the testator's lifetime. Section 85 of the Succession Act, 1965 provides for four circumstances when a will is revoked:

(a) upon the subsequent marriage of the testator except where the will is made in contemplation of the marriage;
(b) upon the execution of a subsequent will or codicil. The subsequent will or codicil should contain a revocation clause revoking all former wills, which establishes the necessary *animus revocandi* for a valid revocation of a will. There is a presumption that a subsequent will revokes a former will. A former will may be partially or wholly revoked by a subsequent will and is determined as a matter of construction of the will by the courts;
(c) by writing and declaring an intention to revoke. Section 85(2) of the Succession Act, 1965 provides that where the testator in writing declares all former wills to be revoked, the writing must be executed in the same manner as a will. The courts strictly apply this requirement;
(d) revocation by destruction occurs by burning, tearing, or destruction of the will by the testator or by someone in the testator's presence and at his or her instruction.

370. Revocation by destruction is provided for in section 85(2) of the Succession Act, 1965. Destruction by revocation requires both the testator to intend to revoke the will and to perform the act of destruction of the will. Where a will is destroyed by mistake, no revocation by destruction occurs. A will may be partially revoked by destruction. The testator must have the same mental capacity to revoke a will as is necessary to execute a will.

371. Where a will is lost and cannot be found, it is presumed that the testator destroyed the will. The presumption is rebuttable and the person alleging the existence of a will must establish that the will was properly executed and establish the contents of the will.

372. A revocation of a will may be conditional upon the happening of some event determined by the testator. Where the revocation is dependent upon some disposition of property, the revocation is called 'dependent relative revocation'. Examples of 'dependent relative revocation' are the purported revocation of a former will on the assumption that a new will was valid, revocation on the mistaken belief that intestacy rules would effect the desired disposition of the deceased's property, and revocation where the testator intends to make a new will but dies prior to executing a new will.

373. Revocation of a subsequent will does not revive a former will. Section 87 of the Succession Act, 1965 requires that for a former will to be revived, it must be re-executed or by a codicil duly executed and demonstrating an intention to revive the former will. The former will must be in existence to be revived and a will that has been revoked by destruction cannot be revived.

§4. Interpretation of Wills

374. Where a court is requested to interpret a will, it is obliged to give effect to the intention of the testator as contained in the will. The primary evidence is the will itself, subject to admitting extrinsic evidence to assist the court in interpreting the will. The following are the general rules of interpretation of wills:

(a) the will is read as a whole whereby a general intention will override a specific intention;
(b) the court will not rewrite a will, as to do otherwise would be to interfere with the testator's right to freely dispose of his property according to his intention. Where, however, a will is unclear, ambiguous or contains an error, the court may make alterations to the will to give effect to the testator's true intention;
(c) words and phrases contained in a will are interpreted according to their ordinary grammatical meaning;
(d) technical terms used by the testator will be presumed to have been used in their technical meaning;
(e) extrinsic evidence may be admitted to explain or clarify the testator's intention, which is provided for in section 90 of the Succession Act, 1965. In *Rowe v.*

Law[200] the Supreme Court stated that section 90 of the Succession Act, 1965 operated to admit extrinsic evidence where it was necessary both to show the intention of the testator and to assist the court in explaining or clarifying any contradiction or ambiguity. This decision has been questioned in *Curtin v. O'Mahony*[201] by the Supreme Court to the extent that extrinsic evidence may be admitted to identify the intention of the testator without there being any ambiguity or contradiction in the will;

(f) inconsistent and contradictory clauses in a will that provide alternative interpretations, one of which would result in the device or bequest failing, are to be interpreted so as to give effect to the device or bequest. This is contained in section 99 of the Succession Act, 1965 and reflects the long established principle known as the 'Golden Rule', which favours testacy over intestacy;

(g) the maxim *falsa demonstratio non nocet cum de corpore constat* operates where there is more than one part in the description of a person or property in a will, and one part is true and identifies the person or property with clarity, the other or false parts may be ignored;

(h) a will speaks from death, a rule which is contained in section 89 of the Succession Act, 1965, the effect of which means that a testator may dispose of any property in his will that he acquires after its execution but before his death. The extent of the testator's property and those who are entitled to inherit under the will are determined as of the date of the testator's death. This is subject to a gift to a person whose identity is established at the date of the execution of the will, rather than at the date of death of the testator. Where there is a gift to a class, the members of the class are determined at the date of death of the testator. These rules are subject to a contrary intention evident in the will;

(i) a testator may make a gift in a will dependent upon the fulfilling of a condition precedent or condition subsequent. The beneficiary will not be vested with the gift unless the condition precedent is fulfilled and likewise will not be entitled to retain the gift unless the condition subsequent is fulfilled. Where the condition is either uncertain, incapable of fulfilment, or contrary to public policy, the condition will be void and the beneficiary may succeed to the gift without having to fulfil the condition. The courts have shown a flexible attitude in relation to conditional gifts, declaring the conditions to be void, particularly where they are restrictive in requiring or prohibiting marriage and marrying persons of the same or different religion;

(j) 'issue' or children for the purposes of the Succession Act, 1965 were originally confined to those children born to the marriage or adopted by the spouses. Illegitimate children were excluded from the definition of 'issue' and were thus incapable of succeeding to the estate of their parent. The rationale for excluding extramarital children from succeeding to the estate of their parent was justified by Article 41 of the Constitution, which would expose the family to attack,

200. [1978] IR 55.
201. [1991] 2 IR 562.

which the State is obliged to protect. The adverse position of non-marital children was confirmed by the Supreme Court in *O'.B. v. S.*[202] The Status of Children Act, 1987 was introduced to provide equal succession rights for all children regardless of the marital relationship of their parents;

(k) foreign wills disposing of property in this jurisdiction and bequests or devises of property, whether movable or immovable, situate in a foreign jurisdiction are interpreted according to the *lex domicilii* of the testator at the date of execution of the will.

§5. Failure of Gifts

375. The following are the reasons why a gift in a will may fail:

(a) disclaimer by deed in writing or implied from the conduct of the beneficiary. A beneficiary may not wish to inherit a particular gift as it may have an onerous condition attached to it or it may carry a liability for which the beneficiary is liable. The beneficiary must disclaim the gift prior to deriving any benefit from it;

(b) a gift may 'lapse' where the beneficiary dies before the testator. Section 91 of the succession Act, 1965 provides that where a gift fails due to 'lapse', the gift may still form part of the testator's estate if the will contains a residuary clause catering for this eventuality. In the absence of such a clause, the lapsed gift is distributed according to the intestacy rules. There are exceptions to the lapse rule:
   - gifts of entails. Section 97 of the Succession Act, 1965 provides that where a testator devises or bequeaths to a beneficiary property for the benefit of the beneficiary during his lifetime and thereafter to the heirs of the beneficiary and the beneficiary dies before the testator, the gift to the heirs of the beneficiary shall not lapse;
   - gifts to children and issue will not lapse where the testator makes in favour of his or her child a gift and the child dies before the testator but is succeeded by his or her own children, the surviving children may succeed to the gift of their parent. Where, however, the gift to the child of the testator is dependent upon the child fulfilling a condition and the child fails to fulfil the condition before predeceasing the testator, the gift will lapse. Unborn children at the death of the testator's child are considered to have been born during the lifetime of the deceased and may succeed to the gift of their deceased parent;
   - discharge of a moral obligation such as an outstanding debt;
   - where the beneficiary dies after the execution of a will but before it is republished, the gift will lapse;

(c) commorientes is provided for in section 5 of the Succession Act, 1965. Where the testator and beneficiary die in the same accident and it is uncertain as to

202. [1984] IR 329.

which of them died first for the purposes of distributing the estate of any of them, it is presumed that they died simultaneously. In this way, neither deceased can inherit from the other and all gifts lapse;

(d) gifts in a will to persons who are witnesses or the spouse of a witness are void by section 82 of the Succession Act, 1965. The rule is subject to a number of exceptions:
   - where the witness and beneficiary is entitled to the payment of a debt from the estate of the testator;
   - where the beneficiary signs the will not as a witness but for example where the beneficiary is also the executor and mistakenly believes that it is necessary to sign the will;
   - where the beneficiary signs the will but inherits the gift as trustee for another;
   - where the witness signs a will and subsequently marries a person in whose favour a gift is made in the will, the gift is not void;
   - where the testator subsequently confirms in a testamentary instrument that a witness to the will is to take the gift in the will;

(e) public policy may prevent a gift in a will taking effect in favour of the beneficiary. Section 120 of the Succession Act, 1965 specifically provides that a beneficiary who commits the crimes of murder or manslaughter of the testator is precluded from taking the gift under the will unless the device or bequest is made by the testator after the offence has been committed. Ireland as yet does not have legislation that enables the court to consider the circumstances under which the testator died at the hands of the beneficiary and to modify the rule that would ordinarily preclude the beneficiary from taking the gift.

There are a number of equitable principles that govern the testamentary dispositions which are as follows:

(a) the rule against perpetuities operates in relation to both *inter vivos* and testamentary dispositions to prevent a gift taking effect where the beneficiary has no control over the future vesting of the property that is the subject matter of the gift. A gift must vest in the beneficiary within a specified period of time that is during the life or lives in being plus twenty-one years and includes the period of gestation;

(b) a gift will fail where the subject matter of the gift or the object of the gift is insufficiently clear to enable the court to give effect to its terms. The courts look favourably upon vague and uncertain gifts and attempt where possible to give effect to a gift. Examples of uncertain gifts that have been given effect are *Makeown v. Ardagh*[203] where the testator bequeathed [blank] a hundred pounds. The court interpreted this as entitling the beneficiary to not less than one hundred pounds and ordered accordingly. Where a testator failed to specify what she bequeathed to three individuals, the court held that she has bequeathed her entire estate between the three equally;

---

203. (1876) IR 10 Eq.

(c) ademption occurs where the subject matter of the gift does not exist at the date of the testator's death and thus the gift cannot take effect;

(d) a gift to a beneficiary who is an unpaid creditor of the testator is presumed to be given the gift in satisfaction of the debt. The presumption arises in parent/ child or other special relationships. A similar presumption, the rule against double portions, arises where a gift is made in a will to a child, and subsequently the testator makes an *inter vivos* gift to the child, the gift in the will is said to be deemed by the *inter vivos* gift;

(e) two gifts in a will to the same beneficiary may raise the presumption that one gift is given in satisfaction or the other or the beneficiary is entitled to both gifts. If the will is silent as to whether the gifts are in substitution of one another or cumulative and where the gifts are of very similar value but not identical, it is presumed that one gift in a will is given in substitution for the other. If the will expressly provides that both gifts are to be taken or if gifts are given in separate instruments, the beneficiary takes both;

(f) where a testator is a joint owner of property and bequeaths or devises his share in that property to the beneficiary who is the other joint owner, the beneficiary, if he or she wishes to take the gift, must take the gift as stated. Where the testator bequeaths or devises property of which he or she is a joint owner and over which he does not have exclusive rights to beneficiaries, one of whom is the other joint owner of the property, that other joint owner is not obliged to give his share of the property to the other beneficiary. If the beneficiary who is also the joint owner of property elects to take the gift, he or she must compensate the other beneficiary for the loss of the value of the gift taken by the joint owner beneficiary. Fundamental to the operation of this rule is the clear intention that testator is attempting in his or her will to dispose of property of which he or she is not the owner;

(g) the rule in *Lawes v. Bennett*[204] provides that where a testator has entered into a contract to purchase land as either vendor or purchaser but dies before the transaction has been completed, the testator's personal representatives are entitled to complete the transaction and the estate of the testator to benefit from that transaction.

§6. Spousal Right

376. Section 111 of the Succession Act, 1965 provides that a surviving spouse with no children is entitled to one-half of the deceased spouse's estate. Where the surviving spouse has children, the right is one-third of the deceased spouse's estate. This right is called the 'legal right' share. It takes priority over all other devices, bequests, and rights on intestacy. The legal right of the surviving spouse takes priority over the rights of creditors. Civil partners and cohabitants who are financially dependent at the date of death may apply for a share from the estate of the deceased by virtue of the Civil Partner and Certain Rights and Obligations of Cohabitants Act, 2010.

204. (1875) 1 Cox 167.

377. A spouse may renounce his or her legal right share in an ante nuptial contract in writing. The legal right share may also be renounced after the marriage of spouses but such must be in writing and made during the lifetime of the other spouse. The latter form of renunciation may be challenged on four grounds of:

(a) undue influence by the other spouse;
(b) ignorance of the contents and effect of the agreement to renounce;
(c) absence of independent legal advice;
(d) the agreement was an improvident or unwise one.

378. The legal right share may be renounced in a separation agreement or extinguished by order of the court in judicial separation or divorce proceedings. Where a decree of divorce has been granted, a spouse no longer has the right to claim the legal right share. Section 18 of the Family Law (Divorce) Act, 1996, however, entitles a spouse for whom proper provision was not made on the grant of a decree of divorce to apply for a share from the deceased spouse's estate. Where a former spouse brings an application for a share from the estate of the deceased spouse, the application must be brought within six months of the granting of representation to the personal representatives of the deceased. The former spouse must give notice to the current surviving spouse of the intention to apply for a share. Only a court may grant the former spouse a share from the deceased spouse's estate, but the amount that a former spouse is entitled to cannot exceed the legal right share. However this right to apply is subject to section 18(10), which provides that the right to apply from the deceased spouse's estate may be extinguished. This is called a 'blocking order' and if it is made, the right to apply from a deceased spouse's estate is absolutely extinguished. A surviving spouse's legal right share is subject to the rules relating to unworthiness to succeed and disinheritance. A spouse, however, may devise or bequeath to a former spouse a share of their estate.

379. A spouse may inherit a share in addition to the legal right share. Where the testator wishes to devise or bequest a share to the surviving spouse that is to be in addition to the legal right share, this must be expressly provided for in the testator's will. In this case, the surviving spouse takes both the legal right share and the bequest under the will. Where there is no express provision as to the effect of a device or bequest in a will, the device or bequest is deemed to be in satisfaction of the legal right share of the surviving spouse.

380. Where a testator dies wholly testate and makes a device or bequest for the surviving spouse in the will, which is not expressly stated to be in addition to the legal right share, the surviving spouse must elect to take the device or bequest as provided for in the will or elect to take the legal right share. Section 115 of the Succession Act, 1965 provides that where the surviving spouse fails to elect, the surviving spouse will be deemed to take under the will and shall not be entitled to take any share as the legal right share. Where a testator dies partly testate and partly intestate, again the surviving spouse must elect to take either:

(a) the legal right share; or

(b) the share on intestacy and any device or bequest under the will.

381. Where the surviving spouse fails to elect, he or she is entitled to take under the intestacy together with any device or bequest under the will. Where a surviving spouse elects to take the device or bequest under the will and that share does not amount to the value of the legal right share, the surviving spouse takes the device or bequest under the will in partial satisfaction of the legal right share. The difference in value between the bequest or device and the legal right share satisfied from the testator's estate. The personal representatives of the testator are obliged to notify the surviving spouse of the right to elect, and the election must be exercised within six months of notification to the spouse or within one year of the first taking out of representation of the testator's estate, whichever is the later. A surviving spouse is not obliged to await notification and may do so prior to the personal representatives giving notice. Where a surviving spouse claims the legal right share, such amounts to an election for the purposes of section 115.

382. The main matrimonial asset is usually the family home and most are held in joint ownership by the spouses. Where one of the spouses dies, the effect of joint ownership is to convey the deceased spouse's half share to the surviving spouse. This operates as a matter of law and is taken by the surviving spouse independently of his or her rights under testate or intestate succession. Where a spouse is not a joint owner of the family home or the deceased has not devised or bequeathed the family home to the surviving spouse, section 56(1) of the Succession Act, 1965 entitles the surviving spouse to request the personal representatives of the deceased spouse to appropriate a dwelling in which the surviving spouse was living at the time of the deceased's death in or towards satisfaction of any share of the surviving spouse. The surviving spouse may also request the appropriation of any household chattels. Where the legal right share of the surviving spouse is inadequate to appropriate the family home and chattels, the share of a child in a bequest or device under a will may be used by the surviving spouse to satisfy the shortfall of the legal right share. The surviving spouse must be a trustee of the infant child of whom the deceased was a parent or acted in loco parentis. The section is silent as to how the surviving spouse holds the interest to the family home and chattels in these circumstances, but it is presumed that the family home is held on trust for himself or herself and the child as tenants in common in proportion to their contributions. In the event that both the legal right share of the surviving spouse and the child's share are inadequate to appropriate the family home, the deficiency may be satisfied by payment in cash to the estate. To avoid hardship, the court has a discretion to order appropriation of the family home to a surviving spouse to avoid hardship.

383. With certain types of property, the right to claim appropriation of the family home is subject to court approval. The court must be satisfied that appropriation is unlikely to diminish the value of the assets of the deceased or to make it more difficult to dispose of them. The onus of proving the unlikely diminution in value rests with the surviving spouse. The application is made by the personal representatives of the deceased under section 56(6) in relation to the following property:

(a) a dwelling that forms part of a building, and an estate or interest in the whole building forms part of the estate;
(b) a dwelling that is held with agricultural land an estate or interest in which forms part of the estate;
(c) where the whole or part of the dwelling was, at the time of the death, used a hotel, guest house, or boarding house;
(d) where part of the dwelling was, at the time of the death, used for purposes other than domestic purposes.

§7. Children's Rights

384. Section 117 of the Succession Act, 1965 confers a judicial discretion to provide for a child from a deceased parent's estate. A child has no fixed legal right share from the deceased parent's estate. Section 117 provides that:

> where the court is of the opinion that the testator has failed in his moral duty to make proper provision for the child in accordance with his means, whether by his will or otherwise, the court may order that such provision shall be made for the child out of the estate as the court thinks just.

385. Any order made in favour of a child cannot affect the legal right share of the surviving spouse, any bequest or device under a will, or any entitlement on intestacy. A child is either a natural child born to a marriage or an adopted child of the deceased. The Status of Children Act, 1987 conferred upon children not born to a marriage the right to apply under this section for a share from the deceased parent's estate. Where the deceased bequeaths his entire estate to the surviving spouse, no application may be brought by a child who must await the death of the surviving spouse and any potential inheritance. The deceased must die testate for an application to be brought by a child. If a deceased dies, intestate no application may be brought. The courts, where possible, will attempt to find that a deceased died testate, which will prevent an injustice arising by the estate being distributed equally amongst the children in equal shares rather than in accordance with the wishes of the deceased.

386. The court considers the application from the perspective of a prudent and just parent. The following are considerations that the courts have considered relevant in deciding section 117 applications:

(a) there must be a positive failure in the moral duty;
(b) that the duty to provide may be fulfilled during the lifetime of the parent in the provision of gifts or an expensive education;
(c) the relationship of parent and child does not of itself impose an obligation to devise or bequeath to a child;
(d) the duty is not to provide adequate provision but proper provision in accordance with the deceased's means;
(e) the value of the device or bequest to the surviving spouse;

(f) the number of children, their ages, health, and positions in life at the time of the deceased's death;
(g) the means of the deceased, which includes immovable property outside the jurisdiction. Where an order is made, it can only relate to property within the jurisdiction;
(h) the age of the child and his or her financial position and prospects in life;
(i) the prior provision by the deceased in favour of the child;
(j) the nature of the relationship between the deceased and the child. In the case of a caring relationship, the court should not interfere with the deceased's testamentary wishes but in the case of a hostile relationship, the court should consider this fact;
(k) the date of valuation of the deceased's estate is the date of death and not the date of execution of the will;
(l) the moral duty of the deceased may include an obligation to elderly and ill parents as well as to children of a former marriage; and
(m) the legal costs incurred by the applicant child in relation to the amount ordered by the court.

387. The assessment of the moral duty is by objective standards but the burden of proof upon the child in bringing the application is said to be a relatively high one. Recently, the Supreme Court has adopted a highly subjective approach to the examination of the parent-child relationship to identify why a child has behaved in particular way towards a parent.[205] The application is heard in chambers with a minimum of formality and expense. An application under section 117 must be brought within twelve months of the first taking out of representation of the deceased's estate. Children under the age of 18 (a minor) are considered as suffering from a disability for the purposes of the Statute of Limitations Acts, 1957 and 1991. These Acts provide for the extension of the limitation period within which actions may be brought. In the case of minors, the general position is that they may bring an action within three years of the disability ceasing. An action under section 117 of the Succession Act, 1965 is a claim independent of a will as it is not made on intestacy and is not a legal right under the Succession Act. Therefore a section 117 application cannot benefit from the extension of time conferred by section 127 of the Succession Act, which provides for a three-year limitation period within which to being a claim in relation to the estate of a deceased person from the date upon which the disability ceases.

§8. Unworthiness to Succeed and Disinheritance

388. Section 120 of the Succession Act provides that any sane person who has been found guilty of the murder, attempted murder, or manslaughter of the deceased is precluded from taking any share in the estate of the deceased unless the deceased made provision for the person in a will after the offence was committed. A person found guilty of one of the above offences is precluded from bringing an application

205. *P.MacD v. MN* [1999] 4 IR 301.

under section 117. Where a spouse is in desertion for two or more years prior to the death of the other spouse, such desertion precludes the spouse from inheriting from the deceased spouse's estate. Desertion occurs where a spouse is shown to have:

(a) separated from the spouse, which can occur whilst the spouses reside in the same house;
(b) intended to voluntarily separate from the other spouse, which excludes such separation arising from hospitalization, imprisonment or foreign employment;
(c) the absence of consent to separate; and
(d) the absence of just cause, which, if present, justifies the spouse leaving and does not amount to desertion. Where a spouse has just cause in leaving the other spouse, the other spouse may be held to be in desertion.

389. Where spouses enter into a separation agreement, such agreements usually provide for the mutual waiving of the spouses' succession rights. On the grant of a judicial separation, the court may extinguish the succession rights of the spouses and in the case of divorce, the right to inherit is extinguished on the grant of a decree of divorce, subject to the right of the spouse to apply from the estate of the deceased spouse, which right can be extinguished under section 18 of the Family Law (Divorce) Act, 1996.

390. Section 121 of the Succession Act provides that where a spouse within three years of his or her death makes a disposition of property, other than a testamentary disposition, which the court considers to have been made for the purpose of defeating or substantially diminishing the share of the surviving spouse and/or children whether under a will or on intestacy, such disposition is deemed to be of no effect. In this case the donee is deemed a debtor of the estate of the deceased in such amount as the court orders. An application under section 121 must be brought within one year from the first taking out of representation of the deceased's estate.

Chapter 4. Acts *Inter Vivos* Related to the Estate

§1. *Inter Vivos* Gifts

391. There are a number of mechanisms whereby property owned by the deceased at his or her death passes to another but not by the will of the deceased and not as part of the deceased's estate.

392. A *donatio mortis causa* is a gift to another person and falls somewhere between an *inter vivos* gift and a testamentary disposition contained in a will. A *donatio mortis causa* operates whereby the donor gives the subject matter of the gift to the donee during his lifetime but the gift only takes effect on the death of the donor. Central to the gift operating is the death of the donee. The gift to the donee must be made in contemplation of the impending death of the donor. If the donor recovers or the donee predeceases the donor, the gift reverts to the donor. The donee may revoke the gift during his lifetime. Most personal property, and it would appear real property, may form the basis a gift. There are three requirements for a valid *donatio mortis causa* to take effect:

(a) the gift must be made in contemplation of death. The donor need not die from the illness that he or she anticipates to die from. Suicide invalidates a *donatio mortis causa*;
(b) the subject matter of the gift must be delivered to the donee with the intention of relinquishing control over the item of property in favour of the donee. The gift may be revoked during the lifetime of the donee but cannot be revoked in the deceased's will as the gift takes effect prior to the will taking effect;
(c) it is intended that the gift takes effect upon the donor's death.

393. The rule in *Strong v. Bird*[206] provides another mechanism whereby property can pass to a party on the death of the deceased but not as part of a bequest or device in the will or as part of the deceased's estate. The rule operates where the subject matter of the gift passes to the donee during the donor's lifetime but that the legal title does not. If the donee is the personal representative of the donor, then all the property of the donor and the legal title to it passes to or vests in the personal representative on the death of the donor, including the gift to the donee. In this way the donee can take the gift on the death of the donor. The rule arose in the context of a debt that was owed to the deceased by the debtor. The debtor was appointed the executor of the deceased's estate, the effect of which released the debtor form the liability to pay the debt. The rule has also been extended to other gifts of property imperfectly made by the deceased to the donee during their lifetime whereby the donee has possession of the property but does not have legal title to it. The appointment of the donee as personal representative of the deceased gives the donee legal title to the property and perfects the gift. The rule operates where it is the intention of the donee to make a gift to the donee. If there is an intention to make

206. (1874) LR 18 Eq 315.

a future gift of the property in the possession of the donee to another person, then the rule does not operate. The intention to make the gift must continue up until the date of death. The rule has also been held to apply to the gifts to administrators where the deceased dies intestate. An administrator is appointed not by the deceased but by operation of law. An administrator who is the donee of property may take the property on being appointed administrator or be relieved of the liability to pay a debt.

394. A secret trust may be utilized to dispose of property on death that is not set out in the will of the deceased. Equity enforced such secret trusts, which were usually made in favour of illegitimate children and mistresses. A secret trust operates where the deceased devises or bequests absolutely property to a beneficiary in his or her will. The deceased, however, secretly communicates with the beneficiary that the devise or bequest is intended to be held on trust by the beneficiary for a third party. Where the beneficiary accepts the trusteeship, the trust will be enforced in favour of the third party. There are three requirements for an effective secret trust:

(a) an intention that the primary beneficiary is to hold the property on trust for the secret beneficiary;
(b) that the intention is communicated to the primary beneficiary. The existence of the secret trust must be communicated to the primary beneficiary during the testator's lifetime but the terms of the trust may be communicated after the death of testator once the primary beneficiary is aware that there are terms relating to the trust; and
(c) the primary beneficiary must accept to hold the property on trust for the secret beneficiary.

395. A final method by which a person may inherit property from the deceased but not under a will and which does not form part of the deceased's estate is where the deceased is the joint owner with another party. On the death of one joint owner under the doctrine of *jus accrescendi*, the property will vest in the other joint owner who becomes the sole legal owner of the property. This usually occurs in relation to the family home between spouses, but other property such as life assurance and pension policies expressly provide for a specified person to benefit from the policy. Bank accounts held in joint names of the deceased and another party do not entitle the surviving joint bank account holder to the monies in the account on the death of the deceased. The monies in the account form part of the estate of the deceased to be distributed in accordance with the will.

396. Persons also may provide for dependents through effecting a life assurance policy and a pension. Life assurance policies are most commonly used in the purchase of property through mortgages where in the event of death, the loan amount outstanding is covered by a policy of insurance taken out to cover the liability remaining on the person's death. It should be noted that in divorce and judicial separation applications, a court can make order in relation to life assurance polices by directing who should benefit from an existing policy or order that a new life assurance policy be taken out to provide for the future financial security of a spouse or dependent member of the family.

397. Pension policies are another method of planning for future financial security. Likewise, in relation to life assurance policies, a court in both divorce and judicial separation proceedings may make orders in relation to existing personal policies determining who is entitled to how much and how much a spouse is entitled to when a pension matures.[207]

§2. Administration of Estates

I. Introduction

398. The estate of a deceased devolves to his personal representatives on his death. The personal representatives administer the estate, which involves the payment of funeral, testamentary, and administration expenses, and the discharge of debts and liabilities of the deceased following which the estate can then be distributed according to the will or on intestacy, as the case may be. The term 'personal representatives' applies to both 'executors' who are named and appointed by the testator in his will and to 'administrators' who are appointed by order of the court where the deceased dies intestate.

399. Where an executor is appointed under a will, the entire estate vests immediately in the executor upon the death of the testator. The executor derives his authority from the will. In the case of an administrator, however, such a person derives his or her authority to administer the estate from the 'letters of administration' granted by a court. There would thus be a lapse in ownership between the deceased dying and the administrator being granted letters of administration. Section 13 of the Succession Act, 1965 provides that in these circumstances the estate of an intestate shall vest in the President of the High Court. The estate of the deceased is protected by vesting it in the President of the High Court prior to grant of letter of administration. The estate of the intestate is further protected by the doctrine of 'relation back', which provides that the grant of administration is related back to the date of the death of the intestate, whereby the administrator of the estate may recover against a wrongdoer in an action for trespass or conversion for the seizure of goods during the period after the death of the intestate but before the grant of administration. The doctrine will not operate where an interest of the intestate has been terminated prior to the grant of administration. Further, an administrator cannot effect a conveyance of the intestate's property prior to the grant of administration, but a purchaser in such circumstances may invoke the equitable principle of 'feeding the estoppel' to obtain legal title to the subject matter of the conveyance.

207. *See* Family Law Act, 1995 and Family Law (Divorce) Act, 1996.

II. Executors and Administrators, Appointment, Duties, and Liabilities

400. A testator may specifically appoint an executor in his will or may confer the power to appoint an executor upon another person. A testator may also nominate a person as a substitute for an executor appointed in the will whereupon after the occurrence of some particular event the appointed executor ceases to act as executor. Such usually occurs where the appointed executor dies prior to the testator. The appointment of an executor by the testator is personal in nature and the appointed executor cannot assign his function to another. A testator may appoint as many executors as he or she wishes, but it is usual practice to appoint two. Order 79 Rule 5(14) of the Rules of the Superior Courts provides that no grant of administration will be granted to more than three persons unless the probate officer directs otherwise. Any person may be appointed an executor by the testator, but where the appointed executor is an infant, administration will be granted to the guardian of the infant but until the infant reaches the age of 18, probate of the will cannot be granted. Where an executor suffers from a disability, whether physical or mental, that impairs his ability to manage his affairs, such a person is precluded from acting as executor during the period of disability. If an executor suffers from a disability after the grant of administration, the grant may be revoked. Where a person is appointed as executor and is of unsound mind, the grant of administration may be made to the committee of the executor. If the executor of unsound mind does not have a committee to act on his or her behalf, the Probate Officer may assign the grant to another person. A corporation may be appointed as executor if it is either a corporation appointed by the High Court to be a trustee and is authorized by its constitution to operate as a trust business and has its place of business in the jurisdiction of the Republic of Ireland or Northern Ireland.

401. An executor is appointed either expressly or by implication. If a person is expressly appointed in a will to act as executor but the identity of the person is unclear, extrinsic evidence may be admitted to clarify the identity of the executor. Where a person is appointed executor by implication, the testator must have expressed a clear intention that the person was to act as executor. Where the testator describes the functions of the person to be appointed as executor in terms applicable to the functions of an executor but describes the office as 'administrator' or 'trustee' rather than 'executor', a court will interpret the wording as intending the appointment of an executor. The appointment of an executor may be conditional on the fulfilling of some condition, such as the death of an executor or refusal of another person to act as the executor.

402. A person nominated as executor is not obliged to act and may renounce the appointment but must do so prior to the grant of probate, after which the executor is fixed with the duties and liabilities of the executor. The renunciation must be in writing, signed by the executor, witnessed, and filed in the Probate Office. The renunciation may be withdrawn but the courts are reluctant to order such unless it is for the benefit of the estate. An executor may be appointed for a limited time and in a limited capacity, but an executor cannot accept only part of his functions and renounce the others. Once an executor is appointed, no other person may act as executor during the grant of probate unless the grant is recalled, revoked, or has expired.

403. The office of executor is accepted by the executor taking out 'probate' of the will. The office also may be accepted by the acts of the executor, which amount to the functions of an executor. Further, a person who is not appointed as the executor in a will but who carries out the functions of an executor by collecting or discharging debts of the testator may be appointed an executor. This person is under a duty to act as executor and assume the liabilities of the office. Such an executor is known as executor *de son tort*. Whether the acts of the executor amount to the exercise of the functions of executor depend upon the circumstances. The publication of notice concerning claims against the estate and taking possession of the goods of the testator have been held to functions of an executor, but burying the deceased and other acts of charity have not.

404. The only person who may take out probate of the testator's will is the appointed executor. Where an executor fails to take out probate, he or she may be summoned by the High Court either to accept or to refuse probate where another person is willing to act as executor. The person willing to act as executor brings a citation requesting the executor either to accept or to refuse probate. If the executor does not enter an appearance to the citation within fourteen days of its issue, the executor will be deemed to have renounced the right to take out probate. Where an executor accepts probate on foot of a citation, the executor is obliged to extract probate within fourteen days. Failure to do so amounts to renouncing the right to take out probate. The right to act as executor is terminated in this way. It is also terminated where the executor dies before taking out probate.

405. Section 22 of the Succession Act, 1965 affords protection to the executor where he or she acts as executor in good faith and in the belief that the grant of probate is valid. Thus the executor is indemnified against any payments or dispositions made on foot of a grant of probate that is invalid or subsequently revoked. If, however, an executor has notice that the grant of probate may be invalid and effects payments or dispositions with such knowledge, the executor may be liable for such if the grant of probate is subsequently revoked. A person who receives payments under a grant of probate that is subsequently revoked is not protected and payments may be recovered. Purchasers who take a conveyance on foot of a grant of probate that is subsequently revoked are protected by section 25 of the Succession Act, 1965. Both the terms 'conveyance' and 'purchaser' are broadly defined in the Act.

406. An executor or administrator is obliged to preserve, protect, and administer the testator's estate, and failure to do so amounts to a wasting of the assets or *devastavit* for which the executor or administrator is personally liable both during his lifetime and after his death against the personal representatives of the deceased executor or administrator. *Devastavit* can occur where the executor or administrator converts assets to his own use by discharging his own personal debts or failure to pay liabilities of the estate from available assets, which incurs additional expense by the creditors bringing an action against the estate.

407. An executor *de son tort* is also liable where he or she acts as executor of the estate. Section 23 of the Succession Act, 1965 provides that any person who defrauds creditors or without full valuable consideration, obtains, receives, or holds any part of the estate or effects the release of any debts or liability due shall be liable for his own wrong to the extent of the estate received or coming into his hands, or for the debt or liability released. An executor *de son tort* is permitted to claim any debt for valuable consideration and without fraud due to him from the estate and any payment made by him that might be made by a personal representative.

III. Grant of Probate

408. Section 26 of the Succession Act, 1965 provides that the Circuit and High Court have concurrent jurisdiction to grant probate to one or more executors named in the will of a deceased person that is subject to the court's power to revoke, cancel, or recall any grant of probate. A grant of probate may be refused where the executor is incapable of acting as executor or where the executor has been found guilty of the murder or manslaughter of the deceased. *In the Goods of Martin Glynn: Ireland and the Attorney General v. Kelly and Concannon*[208] the Supreme Court held that the Chief State Solicitor should be appointed as administrator of the deceased's estate in place of the named executor, Michael Kelly. Michael Kelly had been found guilty of the murder of the testator's sister who had been given a life interest in the testator's farm, and after her death the farm was to pass to Michael Kelly. The Supreme Court held that an ordinary form grant of probate could be given to the Chief State Solicitor rather than a limited form grant of calling in the estate and preserving it until the named executor could apply.

409. A single grant may be made in respect of both real estate and personal estate or separate grants may be made for real estate and personal estate. Section 29 of the Succession Act, 1965 provides that a grant of probate or letters of administration may be made even where the deceased has no estate within the jurisdiction or has left no unadministered estate.

410. The application is made to the Probate Office or the District Probate Registry where the deceased, at the time of his or her death, had a fixed place of residence. The application may be made in person but is common practice to apply through a solicitor. All applications must be made in person and not by post. Where a personal application is made, as opposed to an application by a solicitor, the person applying may not be accompanied by another person unless the Probate Officer or District Registrar otherwise permits. If an application has been the subject of

208. [1992] ILRM 582.

court proceedings, a solicitor must bring the application. The Probate Officer or District Registrar cannot grant probate or letters of administration until all enquiries raised have been answered. In the event of a dispute, the matter is referable to the Circuit or High Court as appropriate.

411. A grant of probate may be in either 'common' form or 'solemn' form. A 'common' form grant of probate arises where there is no contention surrounding the validity of the execution of the will. After the grant of 'common' form probate, the validity of the will may still be challenged. A 'solemn' form probate issues after a court has declared the will to be valid following a probate action. The will cannot be later challenged as to its validity after the grant of probate by order of the court, as such challenge is considered res judicata.

412. A District Probate Registrar grants probate in the name of the High Court. No grant may be made in a contentious case until disposed of or directed by a court. If doubt surrounds the grant of probate, the matter must be sent to the Probate Office for direction by the High Court, which can then direct the Registrar to proceed as directed or to prohibit any further dealing in the matter, in which case the person must apply to the High or Circuit Court for a grant of probate.

413. All applications for a grant of probate, or second and subsequent grants where the sole or last surviving personal representative has died before the administration of the estate is complete, must be notified to the Probate Office. Probate cannot issue until the Probate Office certifies that no other application for probate has been made. A formal warning, a *caveat*, may be entered in the Probate Office, which entitles the person lodging the *caveat* to notice of anything being done in relation to the grant of probate. A *caveat* remains in force for a period of six months and may be renewed. The *caveat* contains the name and address of the person lodging it or the registered place of business of the solicitor who lodges it.

414. A will is granted probate on production of the following documents:

(a) the original will and codicils, if any;
(b) a copy of the will;
(c) an oath of the executor containing his name and address, the name, address, and description of the testator, the date of death, relationship between testator and executor, that the testator did not marry after the making of the will, the gross value of the estate, any court orders, any renunciation by an executor, affidavits of due execution, and the death certificate of the testator;
(d) the Inland Revenue certificate detailing the property of the testator at the time of his or her death, any *inter vivos* transaction made within two years of the testator's death, details of any inheritance received by the testator, the names and addresses of the beneficiaries under the will and the relationship to the executor, any other particulars that the Revenue Commissioners require. A probate tax return form also must be submitted with the Inland Revenue affidavit.

IV. Grant of Administration

415. An administrator is appointed by order of the High Court where the deceased makes a valid will but fails to appoint executors or an appointed executor fails to take out probate. An administrator is also appointed where the deceased dies intestate. Thus a grant of letters of administration may issue with or without the will annexed. An administrator has the same rights and liabilities as an executor.

416. The Rules of the Superior Courts provide for the persons to whom the grant of letters of administration with a will annexed may be made. The priority of these persons is defined in complex and difficult legal terms. In general, the persons who may be appointed an administrator are set in order of priority, and the priority is determined according to the category of the gift bequeathed or devised in the will.

417. Where the deceased dies wholly intestate and there is no will attached to the grant of letters of administration, the person to be appointed administrator is determined in the following order of priority:

(a) the surviving spouse;
(b) the surviving spouse jointly with a child of the deceased nominated by the spouse;
(c) the child or children (legitimated or adopted) of the deceased;
(d) the issue of any child who has died during the lifetime of the deceased;
(e) the father or mother of the deceased;
(f) the brothers and sisters of the deceased (whether of whole or half-blood);
(g) where any brother or sister of the deceased, the children of a predeceased brother or sister;
(h) nephews and nieces of the deceased (whether of whole or half-blood);
(i) grandparents;
(j) uncles and aunts (whether of whole or half-blood);
(k) great grandparents;
(l) other next of kin of nearest degree (whether of whole or half-blood) preferring collaterals to direct lineal ancestors;
(m) the nominee of the State;
(n) creditors.

418. In relation to (a) to (l) above, the personal representative of such persons has the same right to a grant as the person whom he represents. The above order of priority is subject to the court's discretion to grant administration to a person that the court considers fit in the circumstances. Administration may be granted to trust corporations, either solely or jointly with another and to the guardian of a minor until the minor reaches the age of 18. Where a minor has no guardian, the court will appoint a guardian to act as the administrator in place of the minor.

419. Where any legal proceedings are commenced concerning the validity of a will or the obtaining, recalling, or revoking of a grant, the High Court may grant administration to a person who is not party to the proceedings. This is known as administration *pendente lite*, which terminates on the conclusion of the proceedings. An administrator *pendente lite* has the same powers and duties as an administrator but cannot distribute the estate and is subject to the control of the court and any directions made. Another type of temporary grant may be made where the assets of the deceased are liable to waste. This is known as a grant *ad colligenda bona*, which entitles the appointed person to collect and preserve the assets, but the appointed person cannot distribute them until a further grant of administration is made.

420. Special administration may be granted, after the expiration of twelve months from the date of death, where any person appointed an administrator is residing outside the jurisdiction, to a creditor or person with an interest in the estate. Where the court appoints a special administrator who is a party to proceedings, the court may order into court the transfer of monies or securities of the deceased.

421. Where a person is appointed an administrator, he or she must enter into an administration bond for the benefit of the President of the High Court. One or more bonds may be sought and the amount of the bond is usually twice the sworn value of the estate, but the High Court or the Probate Office may seek a lesser sum. The bond must be sworn and attested to by the Probate Officer, District Registrar, or Commissioner for oaths but not by the solicitor or agent of the administrator. If a condition of the bond is broken, the President of the High Court may assign the bond to such person as directed who may recover as trustee for the benefit of all interested persons, the full amount recoverable in relation to the breach of the condition.

422. Where the deceased dies domiciled outside the jurisdiction, a grant of administration intestate or with will attached may be made by the Probate Office to:

(a) the person entrusted with the administration of the moveable estate by the court with jurisdiction in the place where the deceased was domiciled at his death; and
(b) to the person entitled to administer the moveable estate by the law of the place where the deceased was domiciled at his death.

423. In the case of immovable estate, the Probate Office may grant administration intestate, or with will annexed, in accordance with the law that would have been applicable if the deceased had died domiciled in this jurisdiction.

V. Administration of Assets

424. The duty of the personal representatives (executor or administrator) to whom representation has been granted is, after having first discharged funeral expenses and other debts and liabilities of the deceased, to collect all the deceased's assets and distribute them in accordance with the will or the rules of intestacy. There are two types of estate to be distributed, solvent and insolvent.

425. An insolvent estate is one that has insufficient assets to discharge the funeral, testamentary, and administration expenses as well the debts and liabilities of the deceased. Section 46 of the Succession Act, 1965 provides for the discharge of liabilities in the following order of priority:

(a) funeral, testamentary and administration expenses;
(b) secured creditors who have securities such as mortgages, charges or liens over the assets of the deceased;
(c) unsecured creditors are determined according to the bankruptcy laws and preference is given to creditors in the following order of priority:
  - rates and taxes due at the testator's death;
  - wages or salary of a labourer, workman, clerk, or servant in the employment of the deceased for services provided within four months of the deceased's death;
  - sums due in respect of contributions payable in the twelve months prior to the death under social welfare and national insurance legislation.

426. Where the personal representative of the deceased is also a creditor of the deceased, he takes preference to the other creditors in the same class as the personal representative. This is known as the right of retainer to retain debts due to him in preference to other creditors and is provided for in section 46 of the Succession Act, 1965. The right of retainer cannot be exercised where the estate is insolvent.

427. Where the estate is solvent, it is distributed towards the funeral, testamentary, administration, and other debts and liabilities of the deceased. This is subject to the court ordering otherwise and any charges held over the property of the deceased. Creditors of the estate are generally satisfied according to the statutory order of payment for creditors to an insolvent estate. It should be noted that the legal right share of a surviving spouse takes priority over all creditors of the estate. Before a personal representative distributes the estate to those beneficially entitled under the will or on intestacy, the creditors must be given notice to submit their claims on the estate. Once the period specified in the notice has expired, the personal representative may distribute the estate to the beneficiaries. Where the estate is distributed to the beneficiaries, which prevents the creditor being paid by the estate, the creditor may follow the assets of the estate to the beneficiaries and seek payment from them. Once the notice period has expired, the personal representative will not be liable to either the creditor or the beneficiary.

428. The personal representative has one year from the date of death of the deceased to distribute the estate to the beneficiaries. Within one year of the deceased's death, creditors may bring an action for payment against the personal representative. The personal representative transfers the property of the estate to the beneficiaries by assent. In the case of personal property of the deceased, the assent may be informal and implicit by the handing over of physical possession of the item to the beneficiary. In the case of land or real property, a formal assent in writing is necessary for the transfer of legal and equitable interests of real property.

429. The personal representative has the power to sell all or any assets of the estate for the purpose of distributing the estate but the wishes of the beneficiaries must be given effect to, where practicable. In the case of a dispute amongst the beneficiaries, the majority view shall prevail. A purchaser of property from the estate of the deceased is entitled to take the property free from any debt or liability. The personal representative has a broad power conferred by section 55 of the Succession Act, 1965 to appropriate any property of the estate in favour of a beneficiary. The right of the surviving spouse to have the family home appropriated under section 56 is unaffected by the general power of appropriation. No appropriation may occur where such would prejudicially affect a specific device or bequest to a beneficiary. An intended appropriation cannot be effected until notice is given to all persons with an interest in the estate. Where a beneficiary is absolutely entitled to the property, the subject matter of the appropriation, the consent of that beneficiary is necessary for a valid appropriation. The intention of the deceased is paramount in determining whether the personal representative should exercise the power of appropriation.

430. Where an infant is entitled to a share of the estate and there is no trustee appointed to act on behalf of the infant, the personal representative must appoint a trustee and in default must act as trustee for the infant.

431. Section 60 of the Succession Act, 1965 confers upon personal representatives specific powers to deal with the estate of the deceased and they may lease, mortgage, or charge any asset and settle any claim concerning the estate.

432. Any action brought against a personal representative in respect of any claim to the estate of the deceased must be brought within six years from the date on which the right to receive the share or interest accrued.

433. The Finance Act, 1993 introduced a new probate tax of 2% of the taxable value of the deceased's estate. An estate must exceed EUR 10,000 in taxable value before probate tax is payable. The Finance Act 2000 raised the threshold to EUR 50,790. A probate tax return must be sent to the Revenue Commissioners on the filing of the Inland Revenue affidavit. The personal representative is primarily responsible for the probate tax return and the beneficiaries thereafter. The taxable value of the deceased's estate is calculated after the deduction of:

(a) the debts and funeral expenses of the deceased;
(b) 30% of the value of agricultural buildings and land but excluding farm machinery, livestock and bloodstock;
(c) the value of the dwelling house passing to a dependent child or relative;
(d) the value of property given for public or charitable purposes;
(e) the value of superannuation benefits arising on the death of the deceased.

434. Where the surviving spouse takes an absolute interest in property, there is no liability to probate tax.

435. A beneficiary under a will or intestacy may be liable to inheritance tax where the market value of the gift exceeds the stated thresholds. The market value of the property inherited is determined by the price the property would obtain if sold on the open market on the date that the property is valued. The date of valuation is the date on which the executor or administrator is entitled to retain the subject matter of the inheritance for the benefit of the beneficiary.

436. No tax is payable below the threshold amount and the thresholds at which inheritance tax becomes payable are divided into three categories of person as follows:

(a) where the beneficiary is a parent, child, or grandchild under the age of 18 and whose parent is dead, of the deceased;
(b) where the beneficiary is the brother or sister, or child of a brother or sister of the deceased;
(c) where the beneficiary does not fall within (a) or (b) above.

437. The tax payable over the threshold amount is 20%. Liability to inheritance tax arises where either the deceased or the beneficiary is resident within the jurisdiction. If either the deceased or the beneficiary is non-Irish, domiciled, and has not been resident for five consecutive tax years, then no inheritance tax is payable.

§3. TRUSTS

I. Ownership of Property

438. Before the law of trusts is explained, it is first necessary to outline the general principles that govern ownership of property that forms the subject matter of trusts. The term property is divided into two categories, real property or 'realty', which refers to immovable property such as land and buildings and personal property, or 'personalty', which refers to all moveable property. The term personalty is also referred to as 'chattels'.

II. Tenure and the Feudal System

439. Strictly speaking a person does not own land but rather has tenure of an estate or interest in land. Tenure defines the terms and conditions under which a person holds land. An estate in land is defined according to the length or duration for which a person holds the land.

440. The current system by which a person holds land or has tenure is based upon the system introduced by the Anglo-Normans subsequent to the conquest of Ireland in the twelfth century. Anglo-Norman lords were granted land held by the indigenous population. This process continued until the seventeenth century when the 'plantation' of Ireland took place, which resulted in the 'planting' of English and Scottish farmers on land held by the existing land cultivators.

441. The Anglo-Norman system of land ownership was feudal in nature whereby the land was held in a series of hierarchical relations between lords and tenants. The land was held by tenants in return for services. On the death of the tenant or lords, ownership of the land passed to their respective relatives. Each lord owned a piece of land known as a 'manor' which comprised a number of fields that were cultivated by serfs, who provided food for both the lord and for themselves. The serfs at local markets exchanged surplus products of the land. At the apex of this hierarchical system of land ownership or tenure was the King who granted land to his immediate subordinates, the barons, who held tenure as the tenants in chief. The land was in turn granted by the barons to their subordinates through a chain of lords or 'mense lords' ultimately to free and unfree tenants of the lords. All land was held in this form of tenure with a lord presiding, except for Royal manors, which was the only form of absolute ownership of land. Each lord and tenant in the chain of tenure provided services to his superior.

442. The forms of tenure in the feudal system had associated with them various obligations owed by both the lord and the tenant. The incidents of tenure varied according to the type of tenure. The tenant had various obligations to fulfil. These included primogeniture whereby the eldest son of the tenant inherited the tenure on the father's death. If the inheriting son was underage, the lord had the right to stand into the tenure whilst the son was underage. This was known as 'wardship of tenement' and the son was obliged to pay 'relief' to the lord on succeeding to the tenure. During the son's period of underage, the lord had 'wardship of the body', which entitled the lord to arrange the con's marriage and obtain payment from the family of the prospective spouse. The tenant was obliged to swear an oath of loyalty and to pay a form of tax to the lord known as 'aid'. The tenure was terminated on 'escheat', which arose where there was no successor to the tenant or where the tenant committed a felony against the lord. The tenure was also terminated by forfeiture, which arose where the tenant committed treason and the King was entitled to the land. The lord also had obligations to the tenant in the form of 'warranty', which obliged the lord to vouch title to the land where another claimed to have better title than the tenant. In the event that tenant was dispossessed, the lord was obliged to compensate the ousted tenant with a similar grant of tenure. There were three forms of tenure:

(a) Free tenure, which consisted of tenures of Knight Service and Grand Serjeanty where the tenant provided military support for the lord. 'Socage' was also a form of free tenure which involved the tenant providing agricultural services to the lord. In urban areas this was known as 'burgage'. 'Frankalmoin' was the tenure that religious bodies held over land and the obligation to the lord was nominal, which ultimately resulted in religious bodies acquiring large amounts of land.
(b) Unfree tenures were 'villeinage' which became known as 'copyhold' and obliged the tenant to provide labour services to the lord. The tenant could not

transfer the tenure which could only pass to another tenant by a 'surrender' to the lord and 'admittance' to the new tenant. The lord had no power to refuse a transfer of 'copyhold'.

(c) The Anglo-Normans declared illegal the Brehon law of 'gavelkind', which was the Irish system of inheritance whereby all children could inherit, whether legitimate or illegitimate but females could only inherit where there were no sons. The youngest son divided the land and the eldest son had first choice of the divided land. 'Rundale' gave common rights of pasture to local landowners whilst reserving arable lands to the landowners individually but which were occasionally redistributed amongst them. 'Commonage' also concerned common rights of pasture but did not involve any arable land. These rights still exist in the west of Ireland.

443. The feudal system took effect over four centuries commencing with the Anglo-Norman conquest in the twelfth century and taking full effect at the end of the Plantations in the seventeenth century.

444. The creation of tenure or transfer of land in the feudal system arose by 'subinfeudation' where a tenant was granted land by a lord and took legal effect in a ceremony called 'feoffment' where the lord presented land to the tenant, a presentation that was witnessed. The tenant could become lord of his tenant, and so on. Each tenant was obliged to provide the incidents of tenure to the superior lord who could enforce his rights by way of 'distress', which entitled the lord to seize his tenant's chattels. Another form of transfer was 'substitution' where one tenant took the place of the other tenant and owed the incidents of tenure to the overlord. The lord's permission was required for substitution. Where tenure was created in favour of a religious body, this transaction was known as 'mortmain' and rendered the services to the lord valueless. Tenure was terminated by, 'escheat', 'forfeiture', or 'disavowal', which was a denial of title of the lord by the tenant in legal proceedings; 'surrender' by the tenant of his services to the lord, 'mortmain', 'frankalmoin', and failure to perform services.

445. The feudal system of tenure declined with the rise in the monetary value of the products that could be realized from the land. Land in turn acquired a monetary value that was capable of being bought and sold mainly through 'subinfuedation' by tenants who wished to realize the monetary value of their tenure. As the system began to falter, the King introduced the Statute '*Quia Emptores*' of 1290 to halt the decline in the system. '*Quia Emptores*' prohibited the transfer of land by 'subinfeudation' of only fee simple estates (the largest interest in land). A transfer could only arise by substitution but the lord's consent was not necessary. Exemptions from the Statute were necessary at the time of the Plantations. '*Quia Emptores*' ultimately resulted in the decline of the feudal system as lords and tenants transferred lesser interests in land than fee simple estates. With the rise of capitalism in the seventeenth century, feudal tenure was abolished by the Tenures Abolition Act, 1662, which abolished military style tenures and their incidents replacing them with '*free and common socage*' tenures but incidents of such tenures changed from services to rents. The modern term for such tenure is known as 'freehold' land – land held free of any incidents or liabilities.

III. Estates

446. An 'estate' in land is the duration or length of time that a person holds the land. The largest estate in land that a person may hold is a '*fee simple*' estate. A fee simple estate in land may be devised or bequeathed in a will or inherited according to the rules on intestate succession on the death of each successor to the estate. In theory a fee simple estate may be indefinite in duration. A fee simple estate may also be alienated by the owner during their lifetime or create lesser estates in the fee simple.

447. A lesser estate than a fee simple is a '*fee tail*' estate. This estate passes on death to children of the deceased and if any of the children of the deceased are dead at that time to their children. Such estates are rare and were used to keep land within families. A fee tail could not be alienated or disposed by will by the owner. An even lesser estate is a '*life estate*'. Such arises where a person is granted an estate for the duration of their life. A variation of this arises where a person is granted a life estate for the duration of the life of another person. This is known as an estate '*per autre vie*' in which the other person has no interest in the estate and merely provides for the duration for which the person is to have a life estate.

448. A fundamental principle of the law relating to estates is the principle of reversion. Whenever a fee tail or life estate is granted from a fee simple estate, there remains vested in the grantor a part of the fee simple in the *fee tail* or *life estate* that reverts to the grantor when the lesser estate comes to an end. Because a *life estate* or *a fee tail* is lesser than a *fee simple* estate, it must come to an end. When it does it, is said to revert to the grantor or his successors in title. This is known as a '*reversion*'. There is only one theoretical exception to the principle of reversion and that is where land is held by the State, the land is held absolutely and thus the State in these circumstances holds an estate in land greater than a *fee simple*.

IV. Equity and the Development of Trusts

449. Equity, prior to the Judicature (Ireland) Act, 1877, which fused the common law and equity, was administered by the Court of Chancery. Equity as a body of law was developed to counteract the adverse effects of the strict application of the common law, which often resulted in unfair or inequitable results. These adverse results arose because either the action was not recognized by the common law courts or if recognized, could only provide a remedy of damages rather than the more appropriate remedy of the injunction where the dispute concerned the sale of land. The best example of the role of equity was in relation to '*uses*'. A 'use' was the early form of a trust and was utilized by property lawyers to avoid the common law principles relating to the transfer of land. 'Uses' were used to avoid feudal dues or charges, as only the person seized of the land was liable for the dues or charges. 'Uses' were also a method of settling property upon a spouse, a type of property settlement that was not possible at common law, because it was not possible to leave property by will, a landowner could convey his interest in land to a third party who would hold the interest for the benefit of a third party after the death of the landowner.

450. A 'use' operated where A conveys land to B but for the use of C. B was regarded at common law as the legal owner and could alienate the land to the detriment of C. Equity intervened to recognize B's legal interest but subject to the *equitable* interest of C. Owing to the potential for abuse of the system of 'uses' and perhaps more importantly the loss of Royal revenue from feudal dues, the Statute of Uses, 1634 was introduced. The effect of this Act was to execute or enforce the 'use' by vesting the legal interest in the person for whose benefit the 'use' was created (C in the example above). The importance of the Irish Statute of Uses was less than that of the English version a century earlier. By 1634, feudal dues were easily avoided by employing 'uses' that were not executed by the 1634 Act. In that year it became possible to leave land by will.

451. After 1634, various reforms of property law were introduced by statute to simplify the transfer of land. The Statute of Frauds (Ireland) Act, 1695 required transfer of land to be in writing. The modern law of property developed into the coherent body of law with the passing of the Judicature (Ireland) Act, 1877, which co-ordinated the existing common law and equity courts.

V. Trusts

452. A trust is more easily described than defined. It may be described as a relationship recognized by the principles of Equity which arises where property is vested in a person (a trustee) who is obliged to hold the property for the benefit of another person called '*cestui que trust*' or beneficiary. The trustee is the legal owner of the property and the beneficiary, by virtue of the law of equity, is considered to be the beneficial or equitable owner of the property.

453. It can be said that the origin and development of the trust coincided with the establishment and development of the law of equity. By the end of the thirteenth century, the development of the common law was considerable but often harsh and unjust in application. The only remedy for an unfairly treated litigant was to petition the King for a just remedy. This function was delegated to the Lord Chancellor which in time became the Court of Chancery. By the seventeenth century, the Court of Chancery had developed a number of principles upon which it determined disputes before it. This body of law is what today is called 'Equity'. By the nineteenth century, two substantial bodies of law, the common law and equity, had developed alongside one another but the system did not operate effectively until the passing of the Supreme Court of Judicature (Ireland) Act, 1877, which fused both systems.

454. Many principles govern the law of equity that cannot be explained in this text. Perhaps the most important principle that the 1877 Act provided was that where a conflict arose between the application of the common law and equity, then equity would prevail over the common law position.

455. The modern trust evolved from the doctrine of 'uses' that arose where land was given to A for the use of B. The Chancellor would enforce B's right to the benefit of the land by compelling A to hold the land for B's benefit. The appropriate terminology was that A was the legal owner and B the equitable owner of the land. This in essence reflects the modern concept of a trust.

456. A trust is a relationship that arises wherever a person (the trustee) is obliged by equity to hold property, whether real or personal, and whether by legal or equitable title, for the benefit of another person or persons (the beneficiary) or for some object permitted by law, in such a way that the real benefit accrues, not to the trustee, but to the beneficiary or other objects of the trust.

457. The nature of the title to the property by the trustee and the beneficiary is best described as the trustee having nominal ownership and the beneficiary having beneficial ownership. The beneficial ownership of the beneficiary is proprietary in nature in that the interest may be sold, alienated, or disposed by will. If the legal interest in the property, however, comes into the hands of a bona fide purchaser for value without notice of the beneficial interest, then the beneficial interest comes to an end.

VI. Subject Matter of a Trust

458. The subject matter of a trust must be some form of property, either real or personal. It usually takes the form of land or invested funds but it may be money, chattels, equitable interests, or debts. The purpose of the trust may even be charitable. Whatever the subject matter of trust, it must be specified with reasonable certainty in order to take effect.

VII. Classification of Trusts

459. Trusts have been classified and subdivided and the categories are not exclusive in that a trust may arise in more than one category. A trust is classified according to the manner of its creation, the objects that it seeks to benefit, or the nature of the duties imposed on the trustee. The general division is between private and public or charitable trusts. Charitable trusts are ones that are so beneficial to the community and are enforceable by the Attorney General. Private trusts identify the benefit and the person who is to benefit under the trust, two requirements that are necessary for the enforcement of the trust. The main classification of trusts is as follows:

(a) express trusts are created by an express declaration of a settlor or testator by either an *inter vivos* instrument or by will. Certain formalities are required to establish an express trust *inter vivos* or by will. The trust must also be certain as to the words used to execute it, the subject matter of the trust and the beneficiaries. An express trust can be further divided into an executed trust where the trust is declared with precision and requires no further instrument to effect the trust. The other form of express trust is an executory trust, which amounts to a valid trust but which requires a further instrument to give effect to the wishes of the settlor or testator by defining the beneficial interests. A further subdivision arises between completely constituted and incompletely constituted trusts. A completely constituted trust arises when the trust property has been vested in the trustees for the benefit of the beneficiaries;
(b) resulting trusts arise from the unexpressed but presumed intention of the settlor or testator, the effect of which is to result or revert the beneficial interest in the property to the settlor. No formal requirements are necessary to establish such a trust;
(c) constructive trusts arise by operation of law and regardless of the intentions of the parties. The trust is imposed by equity;
(d) simple trusts vest the trust property in the trustee but do not specify what duties the trustee is to perform;
(e) special trusts impose specific duties upon the trustee that he is obliged to perform;
(f) fixed trusts specify the interest in the trust property that each beneficiary is entitled to;
(g) discretionary trusts do not entitle the beneficiary to a specific interest in the trust property, and the share a beneficiary is entitled to is determined according to the trustee's discretion;
(h) protective trusts arise on the happening of an event such as bankruptcy or where the beneficiary attempts to dispose of the trust property.

VIII. Creation of a Trust

460. A trust established by a minor is voidable and may be repudiated during the minor's incapacity, that is, until he reaches the age of 18. Mental incapacity may also affect the ability of a person to establish a trust.

461. Where an express trust is created *inter vivos*, no formalities are required in the case of personal property. In the case of land or real property, section 4 of the Statutes of Fraud (Ireland) Act, 1695 requires that the trust be evidenced in writing. The trust need not be in writing but evidence of the existence of the trust must be in writing. All that is required to establish an *inter vivos* trust of land or real property is to manifest the intention to create the trust. The requirement of the Statute of Frauds will not be imposed where it would deprive a beneficiary of an interest in land. Section 6 of the Statute of Frauds Act, however, provides that where a beneficiary proposes to dispose of an equitable interest in real or personal property held under a trust, such a disposition must be in writing. A trust created by a will must conform to section 78 of the Succession Act, 1965 and must be in writing, signed by the testator, and witnessed.

462. The creation of an express trust does not require any particular wording to effect a valid trust. There are three essential requirements for a valid trust, which are known as the 'three certainties'. These are:

(a) certainty of intention or words. The word 'trust' need not be used to create a trust and the inclusion of the word is not conclusive of a valid trust. A court will examine the substance and effect of the words used to ascertain the intention of the settlor. The words used must establish that the settlor intended to make an absolute gift to the donee which he might in his discretion dispose of according to the wishes of the settlor or alternatively hold the gift on trust;
(b) the subject matter must be certain. Both the subject matter of the trust property and the shares or interests that the beneficiaries are entitled to must be defined with sufficient clarity except where the trust is a discretionary one;
(c) the objects of the trust must be certain. The main reason for this requirement is to enable the trustee or the court to enforce the trust and confer the benefit of the trust upon the beneficiaries. The beneficiaries must be identified or identifiable at the time the trust comes into operation to be a valid trust.

463. A trust must be completely constituted before the beneficiaries can take the benefit of the trust. A trust is completely constituted when the trust property is transferred to the trustees to be held on trust by *inter vivos* deed or by will. The transfer must comply with the formal requirements of the method transfer be it *inter vivos* or by will. An alternative method of completely constituting a trust by transferring the trust property is for the settlor to declare himself a trustee of the property for the benefit of the beneficiaries. The trust itself must manifest that this was the method by which the trust was to be completely constituted. In the case of real property, the declaration of trust must be evidenced in writing. There are exceptions to this rule, which is contained in the equitable principle that 'equity will not perfect an incompletely constituted trust in favour of a volunteer'. The exceptions have been noted in the section on Succession Law and are briefly:

(a) the Rule in *Strong v. Bird* that where an incomplete gift is made during the donor's lifetime and the legal title to the gift subsequently vests in the donee, the donor's prior intention to make the gift is regard as having been perfected provided the intention continues until the donor's death;
(b) a *donatio mortis causa* where the donor delivers the gift to the donee in contemplation of the donor's death, which is conditional upon death and does not take effect until death;
(c) proprietary estoppel arises where the donor knowingly makes a gift to the donee and allows the donee to improve the gift or act to his detriment. In these circumstances, equity will make perfect the imperfect gift.

IX. Trustees

464. The law relating to trustees and their duties and powers are based both in Statute, the Trustee Act, 1893, and in common law principles. A trustee is obliged to perform the duties and obligations provided for in the trust instrument. A trustee should be honest and capable of performing the duties and powers conferred upon him. A trustee may only be remunerated if the trust instrument so provides and may to otherwise profit from the office. If a trustee fails to act, he may be personally liable to the beneficiaries. Any person may be appointed a trustee, even a minor or a corporation, provided that the memorandum and articles of association empower the corporation to so act. There is no minimum or maximum number of trustees that may be appointed, but it is usually practical to appoint at least two or more trustees.

X. Appointment

465. The settlor or testator usually will appoint a trustee by naming the individual in the trust instrument or will as the case may be. In the event that no trustee is appointed or refuses to act or the appointed trustee predeceases the testator or settlor, the court may appoint trustees. Trustees hold the office as joint tenants and where one trustee dies, the surviving trustee acts as trustee, and on the death of the last surviving trustee, the trust property vests in the personal representative of the last surviving trustee until the appointment of new trustees.

466. New or additional trustee may be appointed in accordance with the trust instrument where it so provides. There is also a statutory power to appoint a trustee in section 10 of the Trustee Act, 1893, which must be exercised in writing. The power to statutorily appoint a trustee arises where a trustee:

(a) is dead; or
(b) remains out of the jurisdiction for more than twelve months;
(c) requests to be discharged from the office;
(d) refuses to act; or
(e) is unfit to act or incapable of acting.

467. The power can only be exercised to appoint trustees as replacements, and the number of new trustees may be increased. The power cannot be exercised to appoint additional trustees. An application must be brought to court to appoint additional trustees and can only be made where it appears to the court that it is expedient to do so and would be inexpedient, difficult, or impractical to do so without the assistance of the court.

XI. Retirement

468. A trustee may reject the office of trustee and refuse to carry out the functions. It is recommended that the trustee expresses such intention in writing. Where the trustee accepts the office of trust and has failed to renounce the office within a reasonable time, the trustee can only retire where:

(a) The trust instrument contains an express provision permitting him to do so or all the beneficiaries consent to the trustee retiring from the office.
(b) Section 11 of the Trustee Act, 1893 allows a trustee to retire from the office if the remaining trustees consent in writing to his retirement.
(c) A trustee can retire where a statutory power to appoint new trustees has been exercised.
(d) A trustee may petition the court to appoint new trustees where it is expedient, difficult, or impractical to do so without the court's assistance.

XII. Removal

469. A trustee may be removed from office:

(a) where there is express provision for his removal in the trust instrument or by the beneficiaries;
(b) by the court in exercise of its power under section 25 of the Trustee Act, 1893 in appointing a new trustee where the existing trustee is incapable of acting or refuses to act;
(c) where the trustee acts dishonestly, incompetently, or is deliberately obstructive, the court has an inherent jurisdiction to remove the trustee to protect the beneficiaries;
(d) where the trustee has a conflict of interest between performing his duties and his own personal interests, the court may exercise its inherent jurisdiction to remove a trustee.

XIII. Duties

470. A trustee's duties include:

(a) The first duty a trustee has when appointed is to perform the duties and exercise the powers conferred upon him in accordance with the settlor's or testator's intentions. Thereafter he must ascertain the nature and extent of the trust property. He must also be aware of the nature and extent of the powers conferred upon him. He must ensure that the trust property is vested in him and collect the assets of the trust. He should also investigate whether a former trustee has breached his duty and remedy such.
(b) The trustee should invest the trust property to ensure the beneficiaries are provided with a continuous income but at the same time preserve the capital assets for the benefit of future beneficiaries. An investment only may be made in authorized investments, which is specified in an investment clause in the trust instrument. In this regard the trustee should act with impartiality and prudence.

In certain circumstances, a court may authorize the overriding of an express investment clause where the stated investment would be at variance with the settlor's or testator's intentions. Where there is no express investment clause, a trustee may invest the trust property in accordance with the statutory scheme set out in Part I of the Trustee Act, 1893 as amended by the Trustee (Authorized Investments) Act, 1958. The investments specified are limited and relate to government securities, real securities, stock in semi-state bodies, debentures, or debentures stock in publicly quoted companies registered in Ireland. More recently the list of authorized investments has been extended to include unit trusts, but there is no provision for investment in ordinary equities. The duty of the trustee to act with prudence depends upon whether the trustee is a professional or non-professional trustee. A higher duty of care is required of the professional trustee. The standard expected of a non-professional trustee is that of the ordinary prudent businessman. Where a trustee refuses to invest in a particular investment for personal, social, or political reasons, the trustee will be held to be in breach of his duty.

(c) A trustee must maintain equality between existing and future beneficiaries. This may require the trustee to convert the trust property into some other form and to apportion the beneficiaries' interests. Where the trust instrument specifically obliges the trustee to sell property, the trustee must do so. A trustee is also bound by the rule in *Howe v. Earl of Dartmouth* (1802) 7 Ves 137, which provides that where a will provides for residuary personalty, which is for the benefit of persons who are to enjoy it in succession, the trustee must convert all assets of a wasting, future, or reversionary nature into property of a permanent or income-generating nature. The object of the rule is to ensure that the existing beneficiary does not benefit from wasting assets to the detriment of future beneficiaries whereby the assets may not exist at the time the future beneficiary is to take the benefit of the trust property. Where a duty to convert trust property arises, the trustee must also apportion the trust property for the benefit of the existing and future beneficiaries. Other rules exist as to how the trustee should apportion the existing liabilities and profits of the trust property between existing and future beneficiaries.

(d) A trustee must ascertain the identity of the beneficiaries who are to benefit from the trust and distribute the trust property in accordance with the trust instrument. Curiously, trustees have no statutory power to advertise to identify potential beneficiaries, but personal representatives under the Succession Act, 1965 may advertise. If the whereabouts of a beneficiary is unknown, an application may be brought to court authorizing the distribution of the unknown beneficiary's interest. The application is known as a 'Benjamin order' and may only be applied for after the expiration of seven years. Where a beneficiary receives an under-payment or no payment, the trustee may be liable for breach of his duty. If a doubt arises as to the respective shares of the beneficiaries, the trust may apply to court for direction as to how the trust property should be distributed. If the trustee adheres to the court's directions, he cannot be held liable.

(e) A trustee has a duty to keep accounts and provide information to the beneficiaries. The duty arises from the trustee/beneficiary relationship. The beneficiary has a right to inspect documentation relating only to their interest of the trust property. In the case of a discretionary trust, the beneficiaries are entitled to information relating to the trust property but not to the reasons for the manner in which the trustees exercised their discretion in distributing the trust property unless the beneficiary can establish an improper motive on the trustee's behalf in distributing the trust property.

(f) A trustee may not profit from his office of trustee. He may only be remunerated by the trust if the trust instrument expressly provides. In this regard much depends upon the wording of the trust instrument. A court in exercise of its inherent jurisdiction, however, may authorize the payment to a trustee for the performance of his duties or provide for an additional payment that exceeds the amount provided for in the trust instrument, but only in exception circumstances where the trustee has yielded exceptional profits from investment. Section 25 of the Trustee Act, 1893 provides that a trustee may be reimbursed for all expenses incurred in or about the execution of his trusts or powers. A trustee may not sell trust property to himself and any such sale is voidable at the instance of the beneficiaries. There are exceptions to this rule where the trust instrument provides for a sale of trust property to the trustee, by authorization of a court or where the beneficiaries consent to such. A trustee may purchase trust property from a beneficiary provided that the transaction is fair to the beneficiary and the trustee can show he has not taken advantage of his position and has made full disclosure to the beneficiary.

(g) A trustee cannot delegate his duties and powers to another unless provided for in the trust instrument. Where legal or moral necessity so requires, a trustee may delegate his duties and powers to another trustee. Further, where the proper and prudent administration of the trust so requires, the trustee may appoint an agent, such as a professional trustee, to administer the assets of the trust. The trustee, however, must personally appoint the agent and exercise supervision over the agent.

XIV. Powers

471. The sources of a trustee's powers are primarily found in the trust instrument. The Trustee Act, 1893 also confers statutory powers upon trustees. The powers of trustees are:

(a) to sell property and give receipts. This power may be contained in the trust instrument or be authorized by a court. The exercise of the power of sale obliges the trustee to obtain the best possible price for the trust property. Section 20 of the Trustee Act, 1893 obliges the trustee to provide a written receipt for the sale of any trust property;

(b) to advance payment of income to infant beneficiaries from the trust capital assets;

(c) to compound liabilities under section 21 of the Trustee Act, 1893. This means that a trustee can discharge any debt or liability relating to the trust without any liability for a loss resulting to the trust when the trustee acts in good faith;

(d) to insure any trust property against loss or damage by fire.

472. In limited circumstances, a trustee may vary the express terms of the trust without court approval. Where a beneficiary is of full age, under the rule of *Saunders v. Vautier*,[209] the beneficiary may direct the trustee to transfer the trust property to him and terminate the trust. In limited circumstances, the court also may allow a trustee to depart from the strict terms of the trust instrument where, for example, the beneficiaries are unborn or not of full age and therefore unable to consent to a variation of the trust's terms. A court also has the 'salvage or emergency' jurisdiction to alter a trust instrument where otherwise the trust property would be at risk of loss, destruction, or wasting due to some unforeseen crisis arising for which the settlor or testator had not provided for in the trust instrument. Where a dispute arises between beneficiaries, the court may authorize the trustees to act not in accordance with the trust instrument to compromise the dispute. Finally, a court may direct the payment of maintenance to beneficiaries to be paid out of interest on capital that the trust instrument directed to be accumulated.

XV. Liability

473. A trustee will be in breach of trust where he fails to perform the duties imposed upon him or where he acts in an unauthorized manner. A breach of trust may arise in many ways such as investing trust property in unauthorized investments, failing to distribute the trust property of the beneficiaries or in the incorrect proportions and in failing to exercise proper supervision of an agent. A trustee is personally liable for his breach of trust to the extent of the loss to the trust. He is not generally liable for his co-trustees except where the trustee wilfully disregards his obligations and where he should have intervened to prevent co-trustees breaching their duty. A trustee is only liable for his breach of trust whilst acting as trustee. An action may be brought against a trustee after his death against his personal representatives for a breach of trust committed during his trusteeship. The loss to the trust was assessed at the date the beneficiaries instituted proceedings, but that position changed to the date of judgment. More recently in England, the appropriate date on which to assess the loss to the trust is the highest intermediate value of the loss between date of breach and date of judgment. A trustee is also liable to pay interest on the loss at 8%.

474. Where two or more trustees are held to be in breach of trust, liability is joint and several amongst the trustees. An order for judgment is enforceable against one or all of the trustees, and those against whom the order is enforced may claim a contribution from the other trustees responsible for the breach of trust. Where one trustee acts in a fraudulent manner, that trustee alone will be liable and the other trustees are entitled to an indemnity against liability from the fraudulent trustee for his wrongful acts.

---

209. (1841) Cr & Ph 240.

XVI. Protection Against Liability

475. In limited circumstances, a trustee will be protected against liability for his breach of trust. Where a beneficiary induces, instigates, or participates in a breach of trust by the trustee, the trustee will not be liable. The central issue in such an action by a beneficiary is whether it is fair and equitable that the beneficiary be entitled to bring an action against the trustee where the beneficiary has consented to and benefited from the breach of trust. The beneficiary must be of full age, capacity, and must consent or participate to the breach of trust being fully aware of the facts and circumstances. A court may order a beneficiary to indemnify a trustee where the beneficiary consents or participates in the breach of trust but the loss occasioned to the trust is remedied under section 45 of the Trustee Act, 1893 by impounding the beneficiary's benefit in the trust. A trustee may be absolved of liability by the beneficiaries, subsequently acquiescing in the trustee's breach of duty or by the beneficiaries informally releasing the trustee of liability. If an action for breach of trust is brought six years after the breach, the Statute of Limitations Act, 1957 will operate to bar the action and thus absolve the trustee from liability unless the breach is of a fraudulent nature or the trustee converted trust property or the proceeds of trust property.

XVII. Protection of Beneficiaries and Tracing

476. A trustee will be personally liable to the beneficiaries for a breach of trust resulting in a loss to the beneficiaries. At common law a person wrongfully deprived of his property could follow the property into the hands of another party provided that the property was still identifiable, even if converted, and had not been mixed with other property. This remedy, known as 'tracing', is limited at common law where the property became mixed with other property and was no longer identifiable.

477. Equity, however, provides a wrongfully deprived beneficiary with a substantial remedy against the trustee who acts in breach of duty. The beneficiary can trace the property into the hands of the trustee and if the trustee is insolvent at that time, the beneficiary will take priority against the general creditors of the trustee. Further, where the trustee transfers the beneficiary's trust property to a third party who has no actual or constructive knowledge that the property in his possession is that of the beneficiary, the beneficiary has the right to trace the property into the hands of the innocent third party. The equitable right to trace is based upon a relationship of trust between two persons, otherwise known as a fiduciary relationship. A fiduciary relationship exists between trustee and beneficiary. Unlike at common law, a beneficiary in equity has the right to trace property that becomes mixed with the property of the trustee. Where a beneficiary and another third party's property become mixed, the beneficiary has equal right with the third party.

478. Where the trustee purchases other property with the trust property, the beneficiary has the right to take the purchased property or to secure a charge over the purchased property to the value of the trust property. If the trust property becomes mixed with other property, the beneficiary only has the right to take a charge over the mixed property.

479. The right of a beneficiary to trace will be lost where the trust property cannot be traced or identified. Further, the right is extinguished where the property comes into the hands of a bona fide purchaser for value without notice of the beneficiary's right to trace. Also, a court may prohibit the right to trace where it would be inequitable to do so.

XVIII. Charitable Trusts

480. As a general rule, trusts for a purpose rather than for the benefit of a person are invalid. Charitable trusts are an exception to this rule as they confer a benefit on the public generally. As they are of a public nature, such trusts are enforceable by the Attorney General. The rules relating to certainty of objects do not apply to charitable trusts and such may be enforced even where the objects of the trust are not clearly defined. This is achieved by the 'cy-près' scheme to enable the donor's wishes to be fulfilled as near to the original intention as is possible. Further, the rule against inalienability does not apply to charitable trusts. A charitable trust benefits from exemption from income tax under the Income Tax Act, 1967 and a reduced liability for corporation tax is afforded to any company or corporation established solely for the advancement of religion or education. There are also exemptions for liability to capital gains and capital acquisitions taxes.

481. Charitable trusts are administered by the Commissioners of Charitable Donations and Bequests established by the Charities Act, 1961 who advise charity trustees in relation to the administration of trusts. Charitable trusts fall into four categories known as the Macnaghten classification:

(a) trusts for the relief of poverty;
(b) trusts for the advancement of education;
(c) trusts for the advancement of religion;
(d) trusts for other purposes beneficial to the community.

482. Where property or money is left for charitable purposes but there is no provision for the appointment of trustees, the government is considered to be the trustee. This is known as the 'sign manual' procedure and the government may dispose of the property at its will and pleasure.

XIX. Purpose Trusts

483. Trusts to benefit a purpose other than a charitable one, rather than a person, are generally unenforceable, as there is no person to enforce the trust. The main difficulties with purpose trusts are that they can offend both the rule against perpetuities and the rule against inalienability. If the court is satisfied that both these rules are not offended by the purpose trust, the court will enforce the trust. Moreover, the courts view such trusts as conferring a public benefit and interpret them as valid and enforceable where possible. Where the benefit can be directly or indirectly conferred upon an ascertained or ascertainable individual with sufficient clarity and certainty, such trusts will be upheld. Examples of such purpose trusts are for the erection and maintenance of graves and tombstones and for caring for specified animals. Likewise, trusts for the benefit of unincorporated association, which have no legal personality, may be enforced.

XX. Void and Voidable Trusts

484. A trust may be void at common law where it fails to satisfy statutory requirements or if it is contrary to public policy. Where the trust is void, the trust property is held on a resulting trust for the settlor or in the case of a will. Where a trust creates a future interest the trust is subject to the rule against perpetuities, a rule which requires the trust property to vest in the beneficiary within the life or lives in being plus twenty-one years. Where the property vests outside this period, the trust is void *ab initio.*

485. Where a trust is subject to a condition, either precedent or subsequent, the condition must be fulfilled for the trust to operate. A condition precedent precludes the trust taking effect and a condition subsequent operates to divest the beneficiary of the trust property. Where the condition is considered void, the trust property may vest in the case of a condition subsequent without the application of the condition. In the case of void condition precedent the law is not certain, but there is judicial comment that where the condition is invalid in violating the constitutional rights of the donee, the donee may take the gift without complying with the condition.

486. A trust will be void as offending against public policy if it has as its purpose some illegal or immoral aim. There are two general categories of void trusts where the purpose is to operate as a general restraint on marriage or to interfere with parental duties.

487. A voidable trust takes effect and remains valid until set aside by order of the court. Generally this will occur as a result of mistake, misrepresentation, fraud, duress, or undue influence. Where a trust is established with the intention of defrauding creditors, section 10 of the Conveyancing Act (Ireland), 1634 provides that the gift or conveyance of property is void. Section 1 of the Act provides that any voluntary conveyance made with the intention of defrauding subsequent purchasers is void as against subsequent purchasers.

488. Section 59 of the Bankruptcy Act, 1988 provides that any settlement of property, either real or personal, which is not a settlement before and in consideration of marriage or made in favour of a purchaser in good faith and for valuable consideration, is void as against the official assignee, if the settlor is adjudicated bankrupt within two years of the date of the settlement. If the settlement is made within five years of the settlor being adjudicated bankrupt, the settlement shall be void unless the parties claiming under the settlement prove that the settlor was, at the time of making the settlement, able to pay all his debts without the aid of the property comprised in it and that the interest of the settlor in the settlement property passed to the trustee of the settlement on its execution.

489. In the case of a settlement being void as against the official assignee, this has been interpreted as meaning voidable and requires the official assignee to set aside the settlement. There is no need to prove any fraudulent intent on the settlor's behalf, and the fact of bankruptcy will suffice.

Selected Bibliography

Binchy, W. *Conflict of Laws*. London: Butterworths, 1988.
Brady, J.C. *Succession Law in Ireland*. 2nd ed. Dublin: Butterworths, 1995.
Byrne, R. & P. McCutcheon. *The Irish Legal System*. 4th ed. Dublin: Butterworths, 2001.
Delaney, H. *Equity and the Law of Trusts*. 2nd ed. Dublin: Round Hall/Sweet & Maxwell, 1999.
Keating, A. *Probate Law and Practice in Ireland*. Dublin: Round Hall/Sweet & Maxwell, 1999.
Lyall, A. *Land Law in Ireland*. 2nd ed. Dublin: Round Hall, 2000.
Martin, J.E. (ed.). *Hanbury & Martin Modern Equity*. 15th ed. London: Sweet & Maxwell, 1997.
McDermott, P.A. *Contract Law*. Dublin: Butterworths, 2001.
McMahon, B. & W. Binchy. *Irish Law of Torts*. 3rd ed. Dublin: Butterworths, 2000.
Shatter, A.J. *Shatter's Family Law*. 4th ed. Dublin: Butterworths, 1997.
Ward, P. *The Child Care Act, 1991*. 2nd ed. Dublin: Round Hall, 2005.
Wylie, J.C.W. *Irish Land Law*. 3rd ed. Dublin: Butterworths, 1997.

Selected Bibliography

Index

The numbers given here refer to paragraph numbers.

Index

Index

Index

www.ingramcontent.com/pod-product-compliance
Lightning Source LLC
LaVergne TN
LVHW021108300926
849160LV00009B/652
* 9 7 8 9 4 0 3 5 4 8 9 3 7 *